SOUTHERN AFRICA
The Critical Land

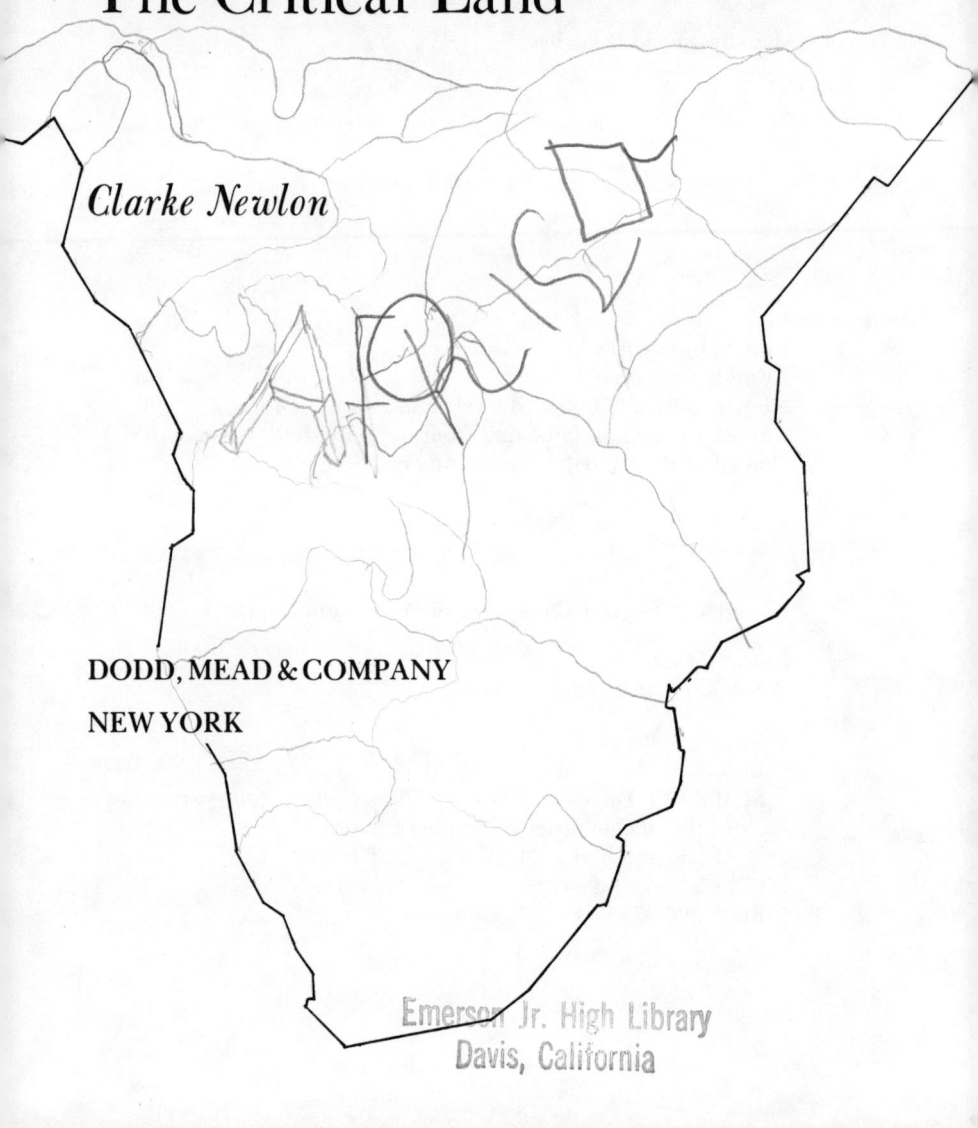

SOUTHERN AFRICA

The Critical Land

Clarke Newlon

DODD, MEAD & COMPANY

NEW YORK

CREDITS FOR PHOTOGRAPHIC SECTION

South African Information Service, numbers 1, 2, 3, 4, 5, 6, 7, 8; Rhodesian Information Office, numbers 9, 10, 11, 12, 13; Zambia Information Services, numbers 14, 16; Swaziland Information Services, numbers 17, 18, 19; Malawi Department of Information, numbers 15, 20, 21, 22, 23, 24.

Maps by Donald T. Pitcher

Library of Congress Cataloging in Publication Data

Newlon, Clarke.
   Southern Africa, the critical land.

   Bibliography: p.
   Includes index.
   SUMMARY: Discusses the history, development, and current problems of the ten countries of Southern Africa.
   1. Africa, Southern.   [1. Africa, Southern]   I. Title.
DT729.5.N48   968   78-7724
ISBN 0-396-07589-4

For Melanie, with love

Contents

List of Illustrations

Following page 128

SOUTHERN AFRICA
The Critical Land

CHAPTER 1

The Strategic Land

THE TEN NATIONS of Southern Africa have been discovered by the rest of the world in just recent years, discovered in the sense that this lower quarter of the world's second largest continent is critically important geographically, economically, politically, and militarily.

Several years ago the Soviet Union cannily recognized the strategic value of the area. The Russians, who previously had shown only a passing interest in it, suddenly moved into the Red Sea with warships. They subsequently tied up two strategically located Southern African countries by political infiltration and the rankly aggressive use of satellite Cuban troops.

Only belatedly did the United States and Western Europe awaken to these realities of international life:

• Half of the world's oil shipping moves around the narrow "Choke Point" of Southern Africa's tip, just off Cape Town.

• An odd half dozen of modern industry's most vitally

important minerals are available to the Western world almost exclusively in the ten nations of Southern Africa.

• The United States has more than a billion and a half dollars invested in Southern Africa, has 6,000 businesses which trade with Southern Africa, and 300 physical U.S.-owned plants there. For Western Europe, particularly Great Britain, those figures would probably have to be doubled.

A highly placed officer on the Southern Africa desk at the Pentagon was mentioning some of the super minerals—chrome, cobalt, platinum, vanadium. "Russia has half the world's supply and Southern Africa the other half," he said. "That isn't quite literally true; it just seems like it when you try to find them."

The ten nations positioned southernmost in Africa are, reading across the map, left to right and down: Angola, Zambia, Malawi, Namibia, Botswana, Rhodesia, Mozambique, South Africa, Swaziland, and Lesotho.

Complicating the economic and strategic picture of this ten-nation bloc is the political situation there. All are technically independent, except that Angola and Mozambique are under the heavy influence of the Soviet Union, and two others, Rhodesia and South Africa, are ruled by a minority of whites who deny any semblance of human rights to the black majorities. The governments of both latter nations exert total apartheid control over the blacks—a condition that South Africa also extends to neighboring Namibia, which she has held in fiefdom since the end of the first World War.

The two—Rhodesia and South Africa—face the disapproval of their African neighbors and the nations of the Western world, which fight a battle of conscience over the moral issue of civil rights and their own strategic and economic interests. In the case of South Africa, by far the richest and most powerful of the ten countries and a flagrant violator of human rights, her protection against economic and financial retaliation has been led for years by the United States—with the not too reluctant help of France and Great Britain.

Late in 1977 the United Nations voted military sanctions against South Africa. It was a rather ineffectual move, since South Africa is already well armed and has the capability to build more of her own weapons, largely under license from the West. The United States joined this boycott of arms sales to make it unanimous in the UN.

When a like attempt was made shortly thereafter to vote complete economic sanctions against South Africa, the United States joined with Britain and France to veto the proposal in the UN Security Council, effectively blocking it. Economic sanctions would have hurt South Africa, but the West as well.

Geographically, Southern Africa is the link between the Indian and the Atlantic oceans and overlooks the passage between the two around the Cape of Good Hope, one of the most heavily traveled sea lanes transporting oil for the Western world.

For centuries the Cape Sea Route has carried the wealth and the raw materials of the East to the industrial nations of the West. Today the cargoes continue, but in

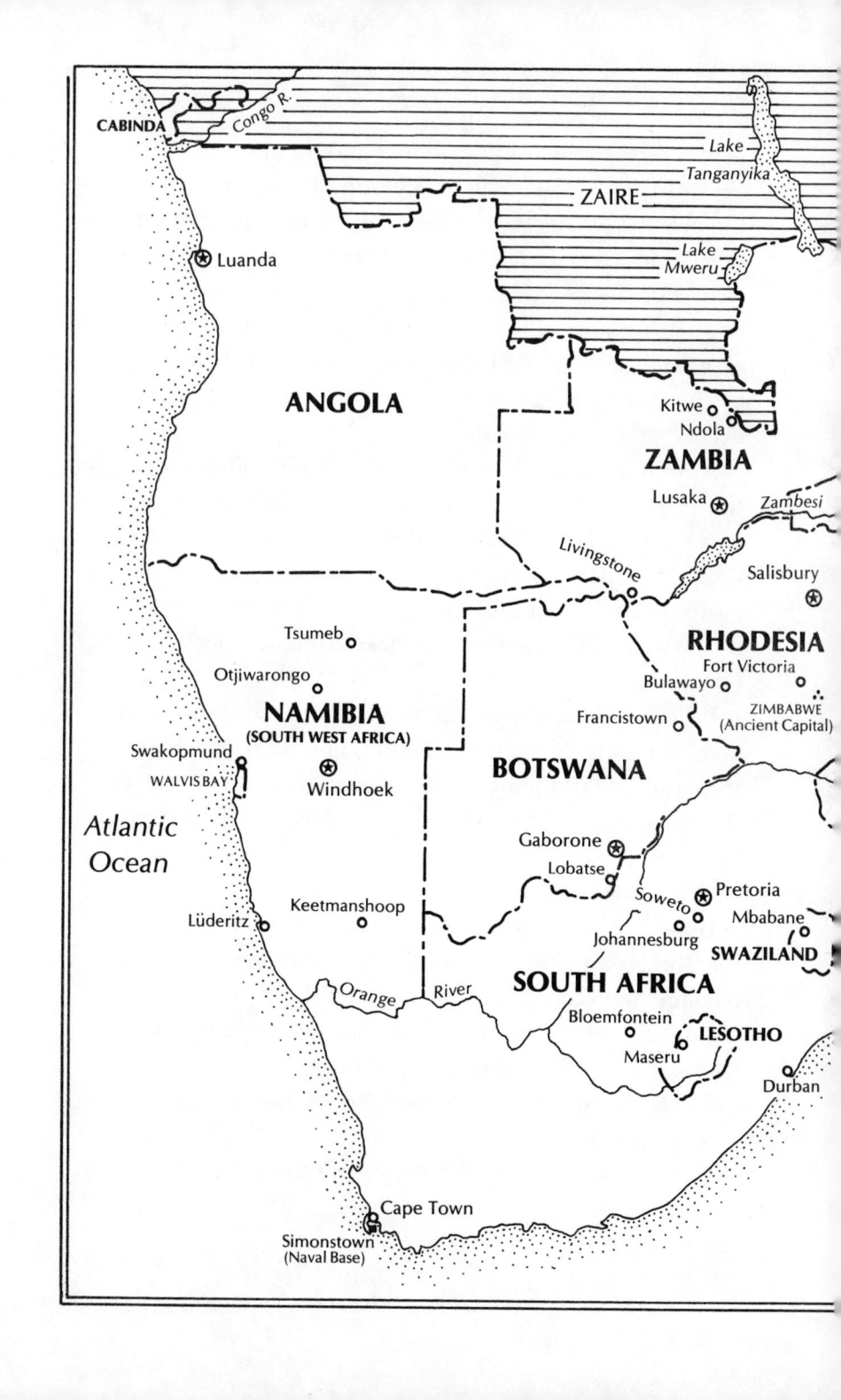

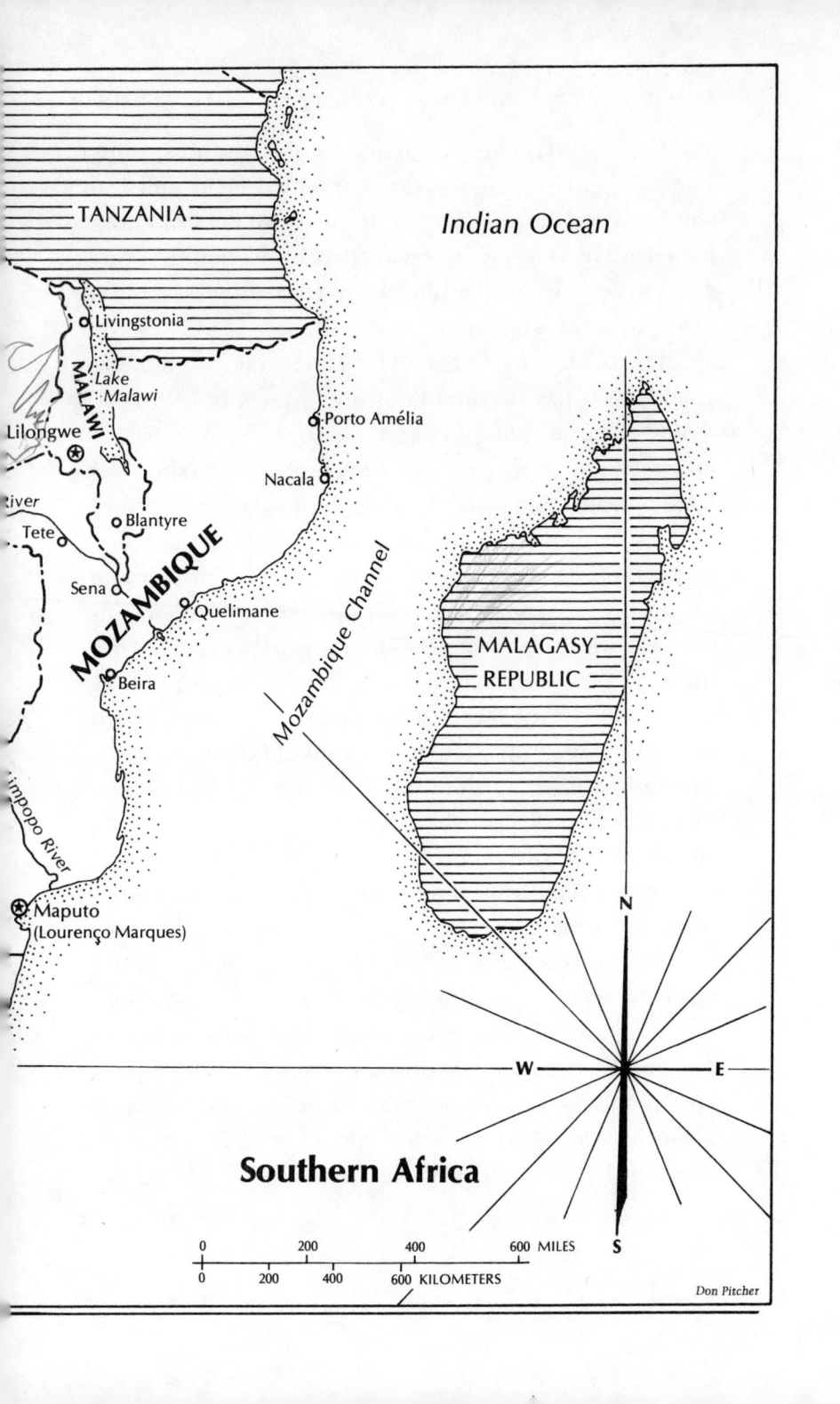

TANZANIA

Indian Ocean

Livingstonia

Lake
Malawi

MALAWI

Lilongwe

Porto Amélia

Nacala

River

Blantyre

Tete

MOZAMBIQUE

Sena

Quelimane

Beira

Mozambique Channel

MALAGASY
REPUBLIC

impopo River

Maputo
(Lourenço Marques)

N

W — E

Southern Africa

S

| 0 | | 200 | | 400 | | 600 MILES |

| 0 | 200 | 400 | | 600 KILOMETERS |

Don Pitcher

addition to the traditional materials, the transport ships also carry oil. Every day of the year between 100 and 150 ships stream down from the Indian Ocean, straddling the island of Malagasy like skiers around a boulder, carried by their own power plus the north-to-south currents of eight to ten knots per hour.

They pass through a narrow strait just off the tip of the Cape which has become known as the "Choke Point" due to the traffic. Ships cling close to the shore because energy and time are precious and close-in is the shortest, fastest route. And also, because the farther from shore a ship steers, the rougher the water gets along this route which the early Portuguese navigators called the "Cape of Storms." Beyond thirty miles out the turbulence increases with every mile—mischievous currents and higher waves, which arrive more frequently, or perhaps just seem to. Out there today's modern tankers would have discomfort; smaller vessels could find it hazardous. The old-time sailing ships made the passage by luck and extraordinary seamanship; often they turned back, sometimes they foundered and were lost.

The key nation in considering any military strategy relating to Southern Africa is, of course, South Africa with her ports and naval base at Simonstown, her critical airfields, and her small but important military strength.

Though hardly impressive in terms of the great powers, South Africa's military forces are by far the strongest among the ten nations of Southern Africa and would be a formidable addition to any allied force. Her military strength by early 1978 figures was: a Navy of two destroyers, seven frigates, seven corvettes, minesweepers, patrol craft, and supply ships, all manned by 5,500 sailors; an Army of about 50,000 full-time personnel equipped with 170 tanks, 1,600 armored cars, 230 armored scout cars, 780 armored personnel carriers, twenty-five 105-mm self-propelled howitzers, seventeen 90-mm antitank guns, and twenty-five additional artillery pieces; an Air Force with 362 combat planes—light bombers, fighters, and interceptors—manned by about 9,000 personnel.

In 1977 the South Africans voted a defense budget increase of 22 percent. The reserve personnel of the three services may reach 300,000 by 1982. South Africa also has the capability of producing a nuclear bomb; in fact, has some tentative plans for testing one in the Kalahari Desert.

It is South Africa's geographical location, however— the commanding position she holds over the Cape Sea Route—which would make her vitally important in case of war, or even in a cold war in which shipping might be interdicted or delayed by one strategem or another.

In this context, military strategists are taking very seriously the almost sudden Russian interest in the African continent, centering in the southern part. The USSR showed little interest in Africa before the late 1960s. There were no Soviet ships in the Indian Ocean before 1967 and very little other activities of any kind. Since then, however, the Soviet Union has established bases in several African countries, including, most importantly, Marxist-led Mozambique on the Indian Ocean, Angola on the Atlantic coast where she maintains a certain amount of control through a proxy army of Cubans, and Guinea-Bissau, the third of the former Portuguese colonies. Early in 1978 the Soviet Union sent their Cubans to help Ethiopia defeat Somalia, a former ally, and win a base on Africa's vital Horn. She maintains a fleet of some twenty ships, half of them military, in the Indian Ocean at all times. The United States finally began stepping up her own activity there in 1977 by the deployment of a nuclear-powered task force, including an aircraft carrier.

Of equal concern, of course, are the Angola-Mozambique locations in Southern Africa. Mozambique on the Indian Ocean flanks South Africa on the northeast. Angola, on the Atlantic, has a long border with Namibia (formerly South West Africa) which the present Angolan government probably considers the equivalent of flanking South Africa, since that nation invaded Angola via Namibia during the recent civil war. In the event of war and under Soviet control, Angola would have a throttlehold on South Africa. Mozambique also shares a common border with Rhodesia, the world's largest chrome producer and exporter.

And, of course, there is the oil which moves around the Cape, and the strategically and economically vital minerals which the United States and the rest of the Western world import from the ten Southern African states. Most of these are shipped from either Cape Town in South Africa or from the Indian Ocean ports higher up.

Major Oil Shipping Routes

AFRICA

Cape of Good Hope

About two billion barrels of oil move around the Cape Sea Route annually, carried by half the world's tanker fleet. Almost half of these ships are too large to use the Suez or the Panama canals. Of the two billion barrels, about 57 percent goes to the nations of Western Europe and 33 percent to the United States. If those to the United States had to go around the Horn of South America, the route would be 5,000 miles longer. It has been estimated that the amount of oil shipped via the Cape Sea Route will have more than doubled by 1980, all coming from the oil-rich nations of the Persian Gulf.

About a quarter of Western Europe's food supplies also pass through the Cape Sea Route.

The United States imports almost all of its chrome, cobalt, and manganese, 80 percent of its platinum, and 36 percent of its vanadium. Of these, the Southern African countries (plus Zaire which is just above Angola in Central Africa) supply: 19 percent of America's platinum, 8 percent of the manganese, 30 percent of the chrome, 57 percent of the vanadium, and 47 percent of the cobalt (from Zaire). America also depends on Southern Africa for gold and industrial and gem diamonds. Western Europe is even more dependent for the above minerals, all of which are vitally important in today's peacetime industry. In event of hostilities, they, like oil, would be critically important. The USSR, with the exception of uranium, is able largely to supply her needs for these minerals from within her own borders.

Not the least of American economic considerations in Southern Africa are her investments there, the bulk of them in the country of South Africa. Some 10 percent of South Africa's capital investment total is from foreign sources. Of this 10 percent, the United States contributes 2 percent—about $1.65 billion. Great Britain's investment total there is much, much larger. The U.S. figure has seen a continual growth for more than a decade, but in the late 1970s showed signs of slowing down some.

Despite the implications of the name, there is very little American money in the Anglo-American Company, the South African conglomerate with tremendous holdings in minerals and other commodities worldwide, including a large share of South Africa's gold production. Anglo-American is closely associated with De Beers, the South African diamond monopoly, with interlocking directorates and sharing the same chairman. The two companies together constitute the nation's most important business interest. The United States does own about 23.3 percent in twenty-three gold mines in South Africa. The ownership is in the form of American Depository Receipts (ADRs). An ADR is similar to a warehouse receipt. It guarantees ownership of a certain number of shares in a certain mining company while the shares themselves may be held in a foreign bank, more or less in escrow. The use of the ADR avoids any conflict with restrictions which may exist on foreign gold holdings.

There are no clear-cut lines to be drawn between military or economic interest and political concern. The United States has a long-time and obvious interest in the more northern countries of the continent—largely political and economic at the moment. In the past few years the American government has been more or less forced to devote an increasing amount of attention to the other areas as well. Part of this is due to world-dimension politics within the United Nations.

There are today fifty-two countries in Africa. All of them are self-governing, and all but three governed—at least technically—at the will of a majority of their people. These three—all in Southern Africa—are South Africa, Namibia, and Rhodesia. In South Africa, 18 percent of the population is white and they rule themselves and also the other 82 percent, black or colored (Indian or mixed); Namibia is, by decree of South Africa, a province of that nation and ruled by South Africa like a fiefdom (although promised freedom at some future date); Rhodesia is a break-away rebel colony of Great Britain, and there the white 5 percent of the population rules in a virtual duplication of South Africa.

If the political lines of Southern Africa seem complex, the indicative nomenclature used for the various people of present-day Southern Africa will appear more so.

Normally, "African" means a black or racially mixed person of black origin. It is both noun and adjective. "Afrikaner" is the term (and spelling) adopted by the white inhabitants of South Africa and Rhodesia of Dutch origin. "Afrikan" is the adjective. The Afrikaners control the apartheid-conscious Nationalist Party which rules South Africa through the government of Prime Minister Balthazar Johannes Vorster. The Afrikaans language is the official language of the country and is taught in the schools, including the segregated black schools, where it is a controversial point; most want tribal and/or English. It is a bastard form of the Dutch language.

The British-descended whites in South Africa, who number about 40 percent of the white population, call themselves "English-speaking," for lack of a better term. This also is true in Rhodesia and most other parts of Southern Africa. The whites in Namibia, formerly South West Africa, who may be of just about any European origin, usually call themselves "Southwesters." To avoid the spoken confusion between "African" and "Afrikan," the Afrikaners some years ago adopted the term "Bantu" for all blacks, because most of the native blacks are members of one of the numerous Bantu tribes. The descriptive adjectives "white" or "black" may prefix any of the nomenclature simply for clarity or emphasis.

All fifty-two of the African nations belong to the United Nations and the majority-ruled forty-nine are all members of the Organization of African Unity and also are identified with the nonaligned nations of the world known as the Third World. (As opposed to the Western world in which the United States has a predominate interest, and the Eastern world where the Soviet Union has an often prevailing influence.) The nonaligned nations have a fluctuating membership of over a hundred out of the UN's total of 149 members. (Djibouti and Vietnam, the last two in, were admitted in 1977.) Obviously the unaligned group constitutes a balance of power between the East and the West and, at times, combines into a solid front to outvote both of them.

In the late 1970s the problems concerning various national governments of Southern Africa were greatly varied: from a lingering civil war and a ruined economy in Angola, to a state of siege mentality in South Africa, to concern that a woman's skirts should not reveal her knees in Malawi.

The former Portuguese colony of Angola certainly had not the least of the area's problems. The MPLA (Popular Movement for the Liberation of Angola), under its military leader and the nation's first president, Agostin Neto, was shakily in charge, with the essential assistance of a hefty Cuban military force. The MPLA held the important coastal areas, the capital of Luanda, and most of the north. The UNITA (Unito Nacional de Independencia Total de Angola) was still very active in the southern areas under its founder and leader, Jonas Savimbi.

In June of 1977 United States Secretary of State Cyrus Vance estimated the number of Cuban troops on Angolan soil by saying that he thought 20,000 "would be a reasonable figure." Later figures placed the number as high as 35,000. Heavily and competently armed by the Soviets, the Cubans held the balance of power between the two factions. UNITA was also receiving some foreign aid, of course—almost certainly from South Africa and Zaire, and possibly from the Chinese. The United States at that time had a firm "no aid" policy set by Congress in December, 1975.

In addition to bolstering the MPLA forces, the Cuban military also guarded the American Gulf Oil Corporation's oil fields on the Angolan appendage of Cabinda, presumably against attack or sabotage from a hostile Zaire and also from the UNITA rebels (whose initial aid had come from the United States). Tiny Cabinda, while part of Angola, is separated from the main body of the nation by the Congo River.

In addition to her precarious military situation, which interests the world, Angola faced acute domestic problems. In 1974, the last year for which figures are available, Angola had a gross national product of just under $3 billion, with imports totaling $541 million and exports a larger $672 million. Of this export total the bulk, $450

million, was in oil, $205 million in coffee, and lesser
amounts in diamonds and iron ore. The United States
was her biggest customer.

Today only the oil remains as an export, under a new
arrangement with Gulf. Oil exports, too, stopped for a
time and then were resumed. Otherwise the country's
economy was brought to a standstill by the civil war.
Coffee was not harvested and the mining operations of
both diamonds and iron ore stopped, due, of course, to
the exodus of 90 percent of the Portuguese population,
which took away technicians, managers, and other workers required to run the economy. The Angolan government was further burdened by the presence of nearly a
quarter million Zaire refugees who had fled the guerrilla
warfare in the Zaire province of Shaba.

Many of the Western nations were reluctant to recognize the MPLA government because of its transparently
Marxist shadings. This was coupled, of course, with the
significant question of just how much influence the Soviet government would permit the Cubans to exert, and
whether or not the Russians would send in their own
military, political, economic, and technical advisors, in-
vited or otherwise.

Mozambique, Portugal's other former colony in
Southern Africa, is much worse off than Angola because
she has no oil under foreign operation as a backstop.
Nationally, the country suffers a balance of payments
deficit, raw material shortage, a stringent lack of credit,
and the loss of all its Portuguese technicians. At the local
level, Portuguese refugees have reported serious food

shortages in the cities, and a return to the barter system. Farmers, unable to get their produce to town because the transportation system has broken down, decline to plant more than their own needs. Many factories have closed because of breakdowns.

Soviet technicians have been sent in to replace some of the most essential Portuguese (who were given a choice of accepting Mozambique citizenship or leaving the country, and largely chose to leave) and there have been complaints that the Russians either cannot cope with the strange machines they encounter or are just plain incompetent. In February of 1976, President Samora Machel admitted that economically his country was "in ruins."

Internationally, Mozambique has been recognized by more than forty other nations but has been slow about establishing any foreign missions, possibly for lack of foreign currency. The United States has an embassy there, but Americans, like other diplomatic representatives, are confined to the capital and not permitted outside the city limits. The number of Soviet technical and otherwise people there has been increasing. And it is possible that here, as in Angola, some of the Portuguese will be brought back through mutual need.

David Kenneth Kaunda became the first President of Zambia, Angola's neighbor on the right, in 1964 at the age of forty and has held the job since. He also is Defense Minister and president of the dominant and only legal political party, the United National Independence Party (UNIP). Zambia was the first of Britain's African territories to become a republic after obtaining independence and is a staunch member of the Commonwealth.

President Kaunda has led his country into a position of both African and Third World leadership. She has remained outside the sphere of influence of either the East or the West and contrives to have excellent relationships with both. The Zambian government is strongly opposed to the apartheid policies which are carried out in South Africa, Namibia, and Rhodesia, and seeks to end her trade with all three—but without great fanfare. Her geographical position makes Zambia an ideal spot for both guerrilla forays into Rhodesia and for peace negotiations as well. She became so angered at one instance of "hot pursuit" by Rhodesian planes over her border that she declared a state of war existed between the two countries.

Zambia and the United States maintain excellent relations. During the early years of the new republic, when her copper economy was in trouble, the United States provided more than $21 million in bilateral economic aid.

Malawi, which lies to the west of Zambia, enjoys the enviable position of being one of the more beautiful countries in Africa and not dominant enough geographically, politically, economically, or strategically to court serious attention from the world's more powerful dominants. Under the President, Dr. H. Kamuzu Banda, her foreign policy direction has been largely toward the West, especially the United States, avoiding any serious contact with the Communist nations. Malawi is a member of the United Nations, of the Organization of African Unity, and of the British Commonwealth.

In contradiction with most of the other Southern African leaders, President Banda does not believe that a policy of isolation (nor embargo or violence) will succeed in altering the policies of the three apartheid countries. Banda maintains pleasant and full diplomatic relations with South Africa, has visited there officially, and received a return call from the South African president.

Namibia, the former South West Africa and another Angolan neighbor, has had no national existence except as an object of dispute between the United Nations and South Africa, which long refused to remove what the UN called "its illegal presence" there. Due to South African policy, Namibia has had no separate representation on any international body. In light of this, the United Nations named a UN Council for Namibia, which has represented the captive territory on the World Health Organization and the UN Educational, Scientific, and Cultural Organization (UNESCO) to which it had been named. The country, where the population is 12 percent white and 88 percent black, has been under colonial or mandate rule since 1883—always apartheid, always repressive toward the native blacks.

Lying between South Africa and Rhodesia, Botswana is known in diplomatic circles as "a front-line state." She abhors the racial policies of South Africa but is closely tied to her powerful neighbor economically. The South African-owned Cape Town-Bulawayo railroad runs for almost 400 miles through Botswana on its way to

Rhodesia. It is vitally important to the country's transportation system and the government has been studying possible ways of buying her part of it with American aid. She has accepted hundreds of Rhodesian refugees; the border between the two countries is officially closed.

Botswana follows the nonaligned policy in international forums and maintains an equally friendly relationship with both the East and West. The United States has given Botswana about $40 million in foreign aid since 1966 and encourages American investment and trade there.

South Africa, whose name has become synonomous with white supremacy and an almost total disregard of human rights, found itself in the last part of the 1970 decade in what even its own people thought of as a state of siege because of its apartheid policies and repressive treatment of the nation's 82 percent black majority. The government of Prime Minister John Vorster seemed prepared to see the beautifully endowed country ravaged by a civil war rather than give the blacks a voice in government policy. Vorster, like other white leaders, preaches delay and a gradual integration of blacks into equal rights. Blacks say it is too late for that.

In the fall of 1977 Prime Minister Vorster dissolved the South African parliament and set new elections for two months later. It was a surprise and predictably successful move to increase the strength of his National Party which already held a considerable majority.

Vorster campaigned against "foreign meddling" and for a new constitution, which both blacks and colored protested because they said it would give them token representation but no real voice in policy.

The "foreign meddling," presumably from the United States and Great Britain, is mostly pure political rhetoric. The United States, with at least the tacit support of Great Britain and the other Western European nations, has taken the lead in holding back sanctions, an embargo, or other economic action against South Africa. Neither the Nixon nor the Ford administrations made serious moves against the Cape country. President Carter's strong advocacy of human rights is reflected in a declaration made in July of 1977 by Secretary of State Vance. Vance called on the Vorster government to break up its apartheid system or face an "inevitable deterioration" in relations with the United States.

No timetable was proposed, however, just that progress must be made toward "an end to racial discrimination and the establishment of full political participation by all South Africans."

This was followed on November 1 by the action of the United States in teaming up with Britain and France to veto three black nation-sponsored resolutions calling for sweeping economic sanctions against South Africa. Canada and West Germany, while not actually joining in the veto, made it clear they agreed. The resolutions were supported by the complete forty-nine-nation black African bloc.

The result of the November 30 election was, as Prime Minister Vorster noted, "not a landslide. It is an avalanche." His National Party gained seventeen seats in parliament, increasing its majority to 134 out of the 165 total. Some of the new members of parliament were far more liberal than their leader and hoped to bring about changes in the nation's rigid apartheid stance. They had attracted votes from some of the more liberal English-speaking, who hope for some new governmental formula which would ease their consciences but not really change things too much while doing so. Yet it was a clear victory for Vorster.

In light of the dependence on the Cape Route which South Africa guards, the vital necessity of the strategic materials from Southern Africa (mostly South Africa), and the considerable investments in Southern Africa (again, mostly South Africa), American policy is obviously pragmatic and temperate. She, along with the other Western nations, is not anxious to throw the land and the economy into chaos by widespread warfare or economic upheaval. The West may not be able to prevent the former but it is very doubtful it would support the second seriously.

The American business policy toward South Africa is spelled out in *Overseas Business Reports,* an official publication of the United States Department of Commerce, of March, 1977, entitled, in fact, "U.S. Government Policy." The statement includes:

"U.S. firms and businessmen trading with South Africa in nonstrategic goods and services are placed under no restrictions peculiar to that country. . . . The United States Government refrains from undertaking in South Africa certain highly visible trade promotion activities, such as trade centers, trade fairs, or specialized trade missions. These restraints on governmental activities do not extend to private U.S. companies and businessmen. . . . The United States neither encourages nor discourages investment in South Africa."

Lesotho and Swaziland, the first of which lies entirely within South Africa and the second almost, maintain friendly relations with their big neighbor. Both deplore the apartheid policy, but both are eminently dependent on South Africa and prefer an appearance, at least, of neutrality.

Swaziland's only other bordering nation is Mozambique, and while the Swazi government is anti-Marxist, its King Sobhuza II occasionally plays one nation against the other. When the King wanted to plan a short rail line from the capital city of Mbabane across Mozambique to the coast he did not ask Mozambique for help, but South Africa.

The United States maintains and seeks to strengthen her good ties to the Swazi with agricultural and educational aid and Peace Corps representatives. Thirty nations have accredited ambassadors to Swaziland, but only the Republic of China, Israel, the United Kingdom, and the United States maintain resident representatives there.

Lesotho is a member of the Commonwealth, the United Nations, and the Organization of African Unity. She identifies strongly with the Third World nonaligned nations and would like very much to become a more influential member of that group. Her relations with South Africa are normally good, but deteriorate occasionally when her big encircling neighbor shows signs of wanting to swallow her up. The present government maintains amiable relations with the West and cheerfully accepts foreign aid, including more than $25 million from the United States over the last decade. And an annual average of 150 Peace Corps volunteers work in secondary education, vocational training, modern farming, and credit union development. Lesotho also labors at bettering international ties with the Arab and East European nations, and the other African states.

In Rhodesia, where a less than 5 percent minority of whites exerts a total control over almost six million blacks, the government in the latter part of the 1970 decade could be classified as an endangered species. Her armed forces were fighting a bitterly ferocious war with rebel guerrillas within her own borders. The United Nations had voted her under stringent sanctions. In addition, the United States and Great Britain combined to exert the heaviest of pressures on the Ian Smith government to abdicate white supremacy and let the country be governed by majority vote. William E. Schaufele, Jr., Assistant Secretary for African Affairs and speaking for the State Department's Office of Southern African Affairs, delineated the American policy with a brief preamble of explanation:

"Probably never in the history of American diplomacy," he said, "has the governmental and public interest, even absorption, in one relatively small and remote area of the world increased at such a rapid pace from quasi-academic to substantial.

"Our concern about Southern Africa is quite unlike

the basis for our interest in other parts of the world important to the United States, such as Europe, the Far East, and the Middle East. Our interest is not strategic. We have consistently made clear that the United States does not wish to play a military role anywhere in Africa. It is also not based on economic interests, although we do want to see that Western Europe as well as the United States retains access to the mineral wealth of Southern Africa. Under the proper political circumstances I can visualize a very substantial growth in two-way trade with that part of the continent."

Then, in September of 1977, Great Britain's Foreign Secretary, David Owen, accompanied by the American Ambassador to the United Nations, Andrew Young, carried to Rhodesia a British seven-point plan outlining how a "surrender of power" by Prime Minister Ian Smith would lead to an independent nation returning to its ancient name of Zimbabwe and to be run by a one-man, one-vote government.

The key points of the Owen Plan were:

1. A surrender of power by the present Rhodesian government and a return to legality. This would mean, of course, returning to her status as a British colony (which status Rhodesia has unilaterally disavowed).

2. An orderly and peaceful transition to independence during 1978.

3. Free and impartial elections on the basis of universal adult suffrage. This would, presumably, bring the blacks to immediate power, since they outnumber the whites about 23 to 1.

4. Establishment of a transitional administration by the British government which would conduct the election. In support of this (and of Point 1) Britain immediately appointed Field Marshal Lord Carver, a former chief of Britain's general staff, as resident commissioner.

5. A peace-keeping force of United Nations troops, an action which would require an order from the UN Security Council.

6. A new constitution featuring an elected government, the end of discrimination, protection of individual rights, and an independent judiciary system.

7. A development fund which would help establish new economic patterns in Rhodesia and raise living standards by providing wider black employment. This point was wrapped in a billion-dollar package which would largely be financed by the United States. Also written into the seven-point proposal were provisions for civil, property, and pension rights for whites to induce them to remain in Rhodesia and help build a new economy.

Only days before the Owen proposal was presented, Smith's all-white Rhodesian Front Party had just completed counting the votes which had given it a clean sweep of all fifty European assembly seats over three all-white opposition parties.

It is doubtful if Smith seriously considered the Owen plan when presented (nor did the Marxist guerrilla leaders). Instead, he spent the next two months in almost daily conference with Rhodesia's three moderate leaders: Bishop Abel Muzorewa, the Rev. Ndabaningi Sithole, and Jeremiah Chirau. Then in February the three announced they had agreed on a formula which would end ninety years of white rule and give the blacks equal voting rights—one man, one vote.

The formula was condemned quickly by other African nations and most of the Western world on the grounds it offered no firm guarantees of black-white equality and excluded the guerrilla leaders.

The United States continued to push for the Owen Plan or some compromise thereof, but found itself seriously embarrassed. If it supported Smith it would be opposing the leaders of the African nations and possibly inviting Cuban intervention. And a refusal to join the moderates meant aiding rebel factions armed and backed by Russia, in effect, actually supporting gains of communism in Africa. (See chapter on Rhodesia.)

CHAPTER 2

The World of Africa

THROUGH THE mist-shrouded shadows of a million years and more, the black African lived in his forests and deserts and savannahs longer than man may have lived anywhere else on earth. For most of those eons, age upon age, it was African living with African through feast and splendor, pestilence and famine, fearing only the simple might of his ravaging neighbor or the anger of the gods of his nightmares.

Then the civilized white man came, bringing sophistications of dread the African had never imagined. He was conquered, abducted, and enslaved, and when that became unfashionable in the civilized world, he was colonized, mandated, and protected, all of which could be translated into semi-slavery under newer terminology.

The first men and women to appear on earth may have evolved in Africa two or three million years ago. Here, in 1959, a British (though African-born) scientist, Dr. Louis Leakey, and his wife Mary made one of the greatest archaeological discoveries of all time: the oldest human skull ever found.

Their encounter with the relic was in the Olduvai Gorge in Tanganyika, before that country joined Zanzibar to become the present United Republic of Tanzania. Tanganyika lies on the East Coast of Africa, between the three lakes of Tanganyika, Nyasa, and Victoria, and the Red Sea, and is just above the ten nations which comprise Southern Africa. In very ancient times Tanzania, and the area surrounding it, was known as Zinj.

The Olduvai Gorge is deep, carved by a river which stormed its way through the narrow walls for centuries and centuries, laying bare also, period upon period of the earth's history.

The Olduvai discovery was made by Mary Leakey in the lower depths of the gorge, merely a fragment of fossilized bone of what appeared to be the mouth structure. Dr. Leakey confirmed his wife's opinion that the fragment was from a human being and the Leakeys then spent months brushing and excavating—with spoons— to collect almost four hundred bone particles which they assembled into virtually a complete skull.

It had enormous teeth and they immediately nicknamed it the "nutcracker." They also gave it the name of *Zinjanthropus,* for the ancient land of Zinj and it later acquired yet a third name, *Homo habilis,* or "able man." For at the same layer of evolution the Leakeys found fossil bits of tools and postulated that their early man both made and used them. Skull and tools were estimated to be about two million years old.

To go back even further—a few billion years—what may have been the first beginnings of life itself were discovered in Southern Africa's Swaziland in 1977. Excavating in a bit of drying swampland on the Umbeluzi River, paleontologist Elso Barghoorn of Harvard University found, he announced later, microscopic fossils of what he judged to be primitive forms of algae. Algae has long been acknowledged as one of earth's earliest forms of life and this find, in the spot which archeologists have named Figtree, was positively dated by subjecting the rock in which the algae were embedded to the same radioactive treatment which determined the age of the moon rocks. Their time on earth was established at three and a half billion years ago, more than a billion years older than any previously found life fossils.

The step from algae to men, then, took something over three billion years, and between even the first man and the known history of man in Africa (or the rest of the world, for that matter), there is a gap of anonymous time which encompasses all but the last ten thousand years— which is only one two-hundredth of man's time on this planet.

Thousands of years ago the Sahara was a land much like today's Middle Western United States—forests with green valleys, rolling hills, and fertile plains. Men of the Stone Age lived there for hundreds—perhaps thousands —of years, hunted the game, ate the berries and roots, carved and painted on the rocks in caves.

When the Sahara withered and dried into the world's largest desert, starting probably about five thousand years ago, many of the inhabitants gradually migrated north and east, establishing the great civilizations of the Sudan and Egypt. They saw great empires and cities built on the shores of the Mediterranean, to be conquered and destroyed and rebuilt scores of times. Other of those early Stone Agers filtered southward to mingle with the tropical tribal peoples of the rain forests and the vast rolling savannahs of Southern Africa.

Africa, with an area of almost twelve million square miles—about three times as large as the United States—is the second largest of all the continents, second only to Asia. The equator cuts it almost exactly in half.

The continent is dominated by a great central plateau notable among other features for spectacular Mount Kilimanjaro at 19,340 feet. In addition to mountains, the plateau also is broken by four great river basins. The Congo lies in the heart of Africa, fed by the waters of the rain forest, and spawns a hundred tributaries. To the north are the river-fed Lake Chad, the seemingly endless Niger, and the historic Nile. The fifth basin, lying to the south, is the Kalahari Desert which has no rivers; in fact, the Kalahari has little water at all. Lake Victoria, which lies on the border between Tanzania and Uganda, is, next to Lake Superior, the largest lake in the world.

The southern half of Africa has the smoothest coastline of any of the continents, one of the reasons it was late in receiving the attention of the white man; they couldn't get ashore. It is also why Africa has a limited fishing industry. Fish do not breed in unprotected waters. Most of Africa's harbors are on the far upper West

Coast in what are the present-day nations of Senegal, Liberia, Guinea, and down the curve to Ghana, Togo, Dahomey, and Nigeria, where the coastal mountains slope gradually to the sea and there are frequent natural harbors. This area was given, appropriately, the term of Slave Coast because of its accessibility to the raiders and traders. The ancestors of most of the black people inhabiting the Western Hemisphere today came from this area, and from Angola.

The North Coast of Africa along the Mediterranean, and the South Coast, comprising what is most of Southern Africa, lie in the temperate zones. It can get uncomfortably chilly in Algeria or in opposing South Africa where it even snows once in a while. But traveling inland from either the northern or southern coast produces the same result—the tropics, where 90 percent of the continent lies. The Sahara occupies more than half of the northern part of the continent, reaching completely across the broad upper half of the land, from Mauritania in the west to Egypt in the east. In the Sahara, as in the southland Kalahari, there is virtually no rainfall, maybe an inch a year. Bordering the desert areas, the climate is dry but not totally arid, producing enough rainfall to water the savannahs and the short grass and stunted trees. The rain forest flourishes in the center of the continent (occupying about 15 percent of it) where the great Congo slogs its way along, fed by tributaries that are like the branches of a giant oak tree. Here the rain is so constant the forest never ceases dripping and the earth never dries completely. The air has a fetid, steamy feel.

It smells unhealthy, and is. Rainfall on both North and South coasts is seasonal and sufficient to support agriculture where the soil permits. The East and West coasts are generally semi-arid.

The native Africans are at least as varied as the people of any other continent, both culturally and linguistically. More than a thousand different groups speak different languages, the groups ranging in size from a few hundred to many millions. These can be divided, depending on the anthropological point of view, into as many as a dozen racial divisions and four or five language divisions.

Of the dozen racial divisions, the black Africans of the ten southern nations contain members of three: the Pygmies, the Bushmen, and the scores and scores of different tribes, groups, and bands which make up the Bantu. These latter come originally from the northern West Coast lands and from a broad area on both sides of the Congo.

Linguistically, the Africans of Southern Africa fall into two groups, the first identified by the use of the Khoisan or "Click" language and the much larger second group, the Congo-Niger classification. The "Click" people—the term comes from the metallic clicking sound incorporated into the pronunciation of many words—include the Pygmies and the Bushmen. The Congo-Niger-speaking Bantu comprise by far the greatest percentage of black Africans living in the ten southern nations.

The African migrants from the Sahara some few thousand years ago found scattered peoples in both the rain forests of the Congo (in which is now Zaire) and the

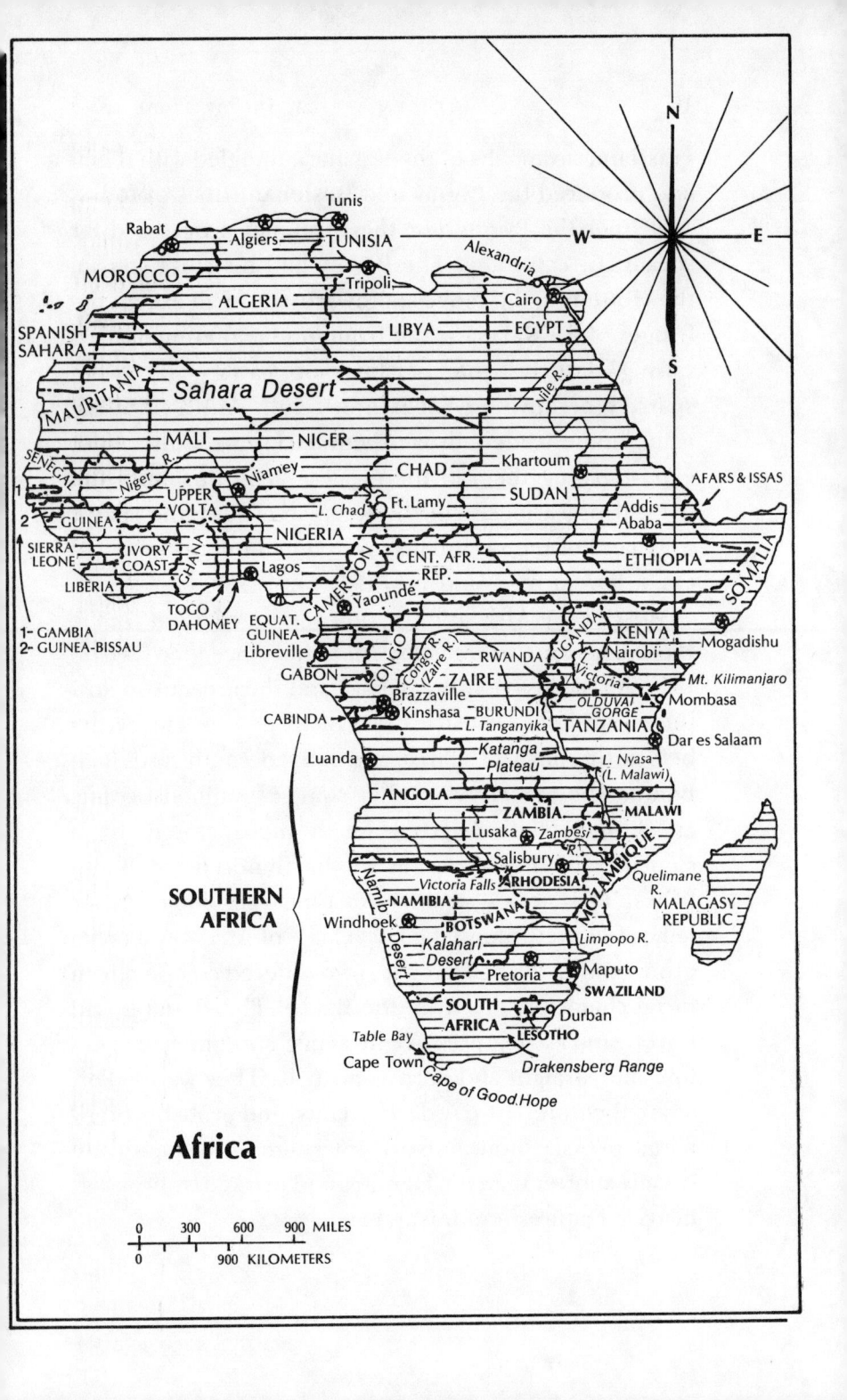

Africa

grassland savannahs of the Kalahari, mingled with them, and produced the Pygmy and Bushman tribes of today.

Neither the Pygmy nor the Bushman progressed far socially or culturally. The Pygmy and his close cousin, the Hottentot, did move southward out of all except the fringes of the Kalahari, and from food gathering to food raising—largely, the herding of cattle—and were sparsely occupying what is now South Africa until the white homesteaders drove them back north, just about exterminating them in the process. The Bushman still lives, if precariously, in the Kalahari, where the sparse grassland of the savannahs are fed by underground rivers, a few springs, and very rare rains.

Most of the African migration was carried out by the Bantu-speaking tribes who probably—since there are no written records—left the Sahara and the area just below the broad hump of Africa two or three thousand years before the birth of Christ and moved southward. The Bantu, who presently number some 50 million people, are linked ethnically, but much more closely by a similarity of the languages of the hundreds of Bantu tribes. They were—in terms of time—accompanied, or led or followed, along the East Coast of Africa by a racial group known as the Hamites, who differed completely in racial characteristics from the Bantu. The Hamites had European-cast features—light skins, straight hair, slim lips, and straight and narrow nostrils. They were taller, as are their present-day descendants, and probably originated in Asia thousands of years ago. The Bantu are usually shorter than the Hamites and marked by broader, heavier features and bushy hair.

The Hamites confined their migration to the East
Coast, although they pushed down as far as present-day
Kenya and Tanzania and are traceable as a race there
today.

The Bantu moved into the Congo basin where they
mixed at least their superior culture with the Pygmies,
and continued on to Southern Africa where they probably ignored the Bushmen. They were strongly en-
trenched as far southwest as present-day Rhodesia and
the Transvaal and the Orange Free State (now provinces
of South Africa) when the white man arrived. This movement of thousands upon thousands of people, linked
largely by language, has been often called the most incredible migration in history.

The ancient great kingdoms which developed, flourished, and died or were supplanted in other parts of the
continent, were largely absent in the southern quarter of
Africa; or if they did exist, they have left no trace. The
one exception, and this did not come until about the
thirteenth century A.D., was in Zimbabwe, now Rhodesia,
and was brought on by the influence of outside trade in
Zimbabwe's gold mines. Here the Shona tribe, members
of the Bantu linguistic group, built the great walled city
of Zimbabwe which flourished as the seat of government
of the nation (see Chapter 7). Later, of course, other
chieftains were able to consolidate their power by tribal
conquests and developed their own comparatively large
kingdoms.

These tribe-over-tribe horizontal power accumula-
tions, which began with the Shona in Zimbabwe, eventually spread to the adjoining areas of what are now South

Africa's provinces of the Transvaal and Natal and the eastern part of the Cape Province, peopled by the Swazi, Xhosa, Venda, and Zulu tribes. None of these bush kingdoms, however, remotely approached the cultural sophistication of Zimbabwe or the advanced civilizations to the north.

There was no private ownership of land among the early Africans. The land was there. It was used as tribal common ground for either cultivation or grazing by long-tenured custom and by the tribal strength to hold it. The only private ownership was of cattle, individual mud huts, and personal possessions: cooking utensils, weapons, clothing, ornaments. The conquest of tribe over tribe may well have been as much social as military, with the cattle-owning tribes holding such a strong caste system superiority over the land cultivators that a natural lord and vassal relationship developed.

Borne along by the great tide of exploration and conquest which obsessed all of Europe's seafaring nations in the middle-teen centuries, Portugal set her eyes on the far coast of Africa. By 1470 the Portuguese had reached the Guineas on the western coast, and in 1488 Bartolomeu Dias had made it as far as the southern tip, now Cape Town. Some ten years later a more daring Vasco da Gama battled his way around the storm-rocked tip, later named the Cape of Good Hope, and sailed into the Indian Ocean, up Africa's southeastern coast, and to India.

Other nations followed, all of them searching for gold or other sources of wealth. The gold was not as great as they had hoped and they turned to another commodity, man himself.

Slavery in one form or another has existed as far back as man's knowledge of himself extends. Man began with the family, then the tribe, and as his life expanded so did his needs and the likelihood that while fulfilling his own requirements he would run into competition with someone else doing the same thing. This led to arguments, and arguments led to physical combat, with the inevitable winner and loser. Usually, in those days, the loser and perhaps his entire family then paid the penalty with bondage to the winner. The ancient cities of Nineveh and Babylon were built largely by captive slaves. The Egyptians prized their Nubian slaves for size and strength, and they also kept the Hebrews in bondage until Moses led them on the forty-year trek back home. The Hebrews themselves had slaves, as did the Romans and the earlier Greeks. In addition to conquered peoples, families frequently sold their children into slavery and sometimes the entire family, to escape total poverty.

Nor was slavery in Africa unknown before the arrival of the white man, though it was usually a modified form, with the slave, most often a conquered neighboring tribesman, being eventually assimilated into the tribe which enslaved him. And, also, his slavery was not hereditary; his children were born free.

The African slave trade began in the fifteenth century, largely carried out along the upper West Coast of Africa. The first slave ship reached North America in 1619 (a few slaves were sold in the West Indies even earlier), and after the discovery that the imported black labor could readily be adapted to the southern climate and was particularly useful for work on farms and plantations there, the trade developed into a vast enterprise which supplied both the United States and Latin America. It was a terribly cruel, degrading form of commerce, which lasted until the nineteenth century. Millions of blacks were shipped to the American continent from the West Coast of Africa. Angola was the chief target in Southern Africa. Then under Portuguese rule, the country saw hundreds of thousands of its men, women, and children herded to the ports by African chieftains (who were paid largely in cheap cloth, knives, and trinkets), held in stockades and then crammed aboard virulent slave ships for transport to labor on the southern farms of the United States or in the mines of Latin America. The descendants of the African slaves shipped to the Americas—the number has been estimated all the way from fifteen to fifty million—make up the black populations of the nations of the Americas today.

Outside of the area around the Cape where the British and the Dutch were both putting down firm roots, there was little real African involvement by the European powers until about 1880, and then the age of colonization came on with a giant surge. Part of the rush to acquire colonies in the so-called "Dark Continent" may have been due to economics. Mostly, however, it was due much more to a follow-the-leader act and then political check and checkmate. If one power was there, the others had to be too.

Leopold II of Belgium pushed what had been a mere show of interest into a giant colony fever in 1885 when he annexed, as a personal land holding, the Congo. It was an area thirty-five times as large as Belgium, the nation he ruled legitimately. Portugal, which had already laid her tenuous claims to Angola, Mozambique, and Portuguese Guinea, proceeded to reassert her claims to these territories. France acquired her immense Northwest African empire, plus Equatorial Africa north of the Congo. Germany staked out South West Africa, Kamerun (the Cameroons), and Togoland on the West Coast, and German East Africa on the East. Britain consolidated her grip on the Cape area by taking over Northern Rhodesia and Bechuanaland (now Botswana and Zambia), plus Southern Rhodesia, (now just Rhodesia). She also held British East Africa. Spain claimed the Canary Islands and tiny Rio de Oro, later the Spanish Sahara. Italy was established in Libya and Eritrea. The French, British, and Italians divided up Somaliland.

Thus by 1914 and the beginning of World War I, only two countries in all of Africa could claim independence, Ethiopia and Egypt. The latter was more in name than in actuality. The British had been "occupying" Egypt since 1882 and continued to oversee Egyptian affairs until they were finally pushed out well after World War II. Ethiopia was ruled by a line of kings she traced back by pleasant legend to King Solomon and the Queen of Sheba. This African colonial era lasted half a century.

The effect of colonial rule can be debated endlessly. Nations are not born equal and no one pretends that they are. The Western world has always used its own way of life and culture as a measuring stick when it regarded the people of other nations. And, by their own standards, Westerners have always regarded native Africans as either undeveloped (or underdeveloped, when they wanted to soften the term).

If the Africans had a voice loud enough to be heard in this matter, they probably would prefer to be measured in light of their own cultures. And to point out that in terms of the lines along which their culture has developed, in view of their own history and not that of another world, they are neither undeveloped nor underdeveloped. They have simply developed differently.

All nations differ in their methods of colonial rule. The British preferred to deal with the people through their own leaders, though keeping firm control over important policy making. The French set up their own governing officials, frequently down to a fairly low level. The Belgians, after the government took over from Leopold's private company in 1909, ran the Congo competently, much as the French. The Portuguese made great pretenses; qualified natives were given "equal rights" of citizenship with the colonial masters. The trouble was that only a miniscule number of natives were ever able to qualify. The British tended to think in terms of eventual independence for their colonies, as the French and Belgians rarely did. The Germans were rigid behaviorists but otherwise were neither better nor worse than most of the colonizers of their day and time.

None of the colonizers, however—not the British,

French, Belgian, nor Italian—made any effort to raise the level of technical education of the people they took over and on whom they imposed a new cultural structure. At no time—nor has the situation changed much in the three remaining white-ruled states—did the ruling officials attempt to educate the native labor forces up to a technical level approaching their own. The native Africans were always used as cheap, unskilled labor. Sometimes their children were educated, but schooling usually stopped at the primary level. (Portuguese South West Africa produced one native black college graduate in something like a dozen years.)

Paradoxically, under colonialism the natives still were often better served—in terms of assured jobs, a better diet, better medical care, and even better education—than they had been in a former existence. This is true now in the three white-ruled countries of Southern Africa.

The Africans are not, however, as their own leaders sometimes point out, better served in terms of their own culture and development because they have not been independent so that they could develop along the lines that their own culture would have led them. They cannot but be conscious of the humility of being ruled by a tiny foreign minority, even under the most benign form of colonialism. The most liberal foreign rule does not equal the freedom to make your own decisions, including mistakes, or to rule your own life as free men and women.

The surge for independence began after World War II. Many black Africans had served beside the white man in the military and had seen him both in victory and defeat. Mostly he had learned that the white man was sometimes a hero and sometimes not, but definitely not invincible. Also, more blacks were going out of the country for education. They were beginning to rebel at the colonial system of dual pay rates for the same job, less for the black. And they were developing leaders.

The first European power to grant independence was Britain in 1957 to the Gold Coast, which promptly renamed itself the Republic of Ghana and elected Kwame Nkrumah its first president. The following year France's President Charles de Gaulle gave the French colonies the choice of independence or of self-government while still remaining "in the family." French Guinea was the first to choose independence, with other French colonies below the Sahara quickly following suit. In 1960 the Belgians bowed to the inevitable and granted the Congo complete freedom. At that time, after almost a century of colonial rule, the Congo (now Zaire) had only sixteen or seventeen college graduates out of a black population of fourteen million.

The end of absentee colonial rule came on June 27, 1977, when the tiny French territory of Afars and Issas, more commonly known as Djibouti, the name of the capital, voted more than 98 percent for independence. The little country, poor by any standard and its nomadic people racially divided, is highly coveted by its adjoining neighbors, Somalia and Ethiopia. Ethiopia particularly needs the port city of Djibouti. It is her only outlet to the Gulf of Aden.

Thus, in late 1970, forty-nine of Africa's fifty-two countries had achieved self-government by the majority, which means, of course, by the black Africans. Independence has not been all good by any means. It is a time of experiment, and many of the people are experiencing the results of the years during which their countries were moved from agrarianism to the industrial age, while they were taken along only as spectators. And they are learning also about the social, economic, and fiscal complexities of internal government and external commerce and relations.

Some of the results have been very good. Others range from merely bad to horrifying. Even at the worst, however, they have not outdone the Western world on occasions, some within memory.

While this was happening, in the other three countries —South Africa, Namibia, and Rhodesia—the white minorities clung to the nearly absolute controls they have exercised for so many years. As the pressures increased, however, it became apparent that eventually the whites must bow to the inevitable. It was a matter of not whether, but when, and peacefully or by blood-stained rebellion.

CHAPTER 3

The Diamonds

DIAMONDS ARE the best friend of anyone who has them. In today's world that anyone is preeminently De Beers Consolidated Mines, Ltd., whose sales of this hardest, most precious gem are approaching the billion-dollar-a-year mark if they haven't surpassed it.

The name of De Beers is synonymous with diamonds. The company mines most of the diamonds from both South Africa and Namibia (South West Africa) and has the right to purchase all of the diamonds mined in neighboring Rhodesia. Together, this accounts for about 40 percent of the world's supply, maybe a little more. De Beers then buys up all other available diamonds, probably another 45 percent, giving the firm wholesale ownership of about 85 percent of the world's diamonds. In addition, Russia, which has a sizeable production of excellent stones, also markets through De Beers, although neither the Russians nor the firm will talk about it. Thus, the actual marketing control De Beers achieves over the world's supply of diamonds approaches 100 percent.

The statistics of diamond production are engrossing. The story of the diamond itself and the charm and fascination it has held for women over the centuries is even more so.

A few years back thousands of New Yorkers lined up for hours along Fifth Avenue in a cold October drizzle to see, through unbreakable glass and under the supervision of armed guards, the 69.42-carat diamond which Richard Burton had bought as a present for his wife, Elizabeth Taylor. The stone was displayed at Tiffany's who had sold it to Burton at a reported price of one million fifty thousand dollars. The purchase was made partly because Elizabeth collects diamonds, and partly (probably) because the resulting publicity which accrued to the two film stars may well have been worth a million dollars.

Diamonds have always charmed women. For ages, their husbands, friends, and lovers have been well aware of this and frequently generous. Elizabeth I started the trend in England by decorating herself with quantities of diamonds, most of them presented by the Earl of Leicester. The trend continued. Henrietta Maria, sister of France's King Louis XIII, brought her own diamonds when she married Charles I, King of England, Scotland, and Ireland around 1626. Lady Hamilton, of some notoriety in her own period, reportedly bought almost three-quarters of a million dollars worth on a trip to New York, charging them casually to her husband. Empress Eugenie, the famed Spanish beauty and consort of Napoleon

III, took her diamonds along when she fled to England in 1870 during the Franco-Prussian War. Among them was the stone, the Empress Eugenie, a 51-carat, oval-cut stone which had been a wedding gift from her famous husband. Wallie Simpson, who was to become the Duchess of Windsor, started the London vogue of wearing big diamond sprays, frequently having dresses designed to complement them. England's present Queen Elizabeth II contents herself with an occasional unostentatious wearing of the crown jewels.

The love of owning and wearing diamonds has by no means been limited to women. The great moguls of the Moslem Empire of India wore them as rings, on pendants, and as turban ornaments. And one of the reasons the Western world was so tardy in its knowledge and appreciation of the stone was because the rulers of the Middle Eastern states intercepted and bought most of the better diamonds from the early-day Indian traders. In America, James Buchanan Brady, of prodigious wealth and appetite, was a great philanthropist, a multimillionaire who endowed hospitals. But he was, and is, better known as "Diamond Jim" Brady, both for collecting the gems and for wearing them.

The high prestige of the diamond is based on its physical properties or beauty and on its record through the ages as a valuable and durable physical commodity in the marketplace. This was true once because the diamond was an absolute rarity. It continues today because while the diamond is still comparatively rare (the ruby and emerald are both more so) that rarity is heightened and maintained by the monopoly which controls its production and sale.

Physically, the diamond is, of course, a mineral. Chemically, it is almost pure carbon in crystalline form and a product of the earth, formed by the forces of nature. Largely from a study of the terrestrial conditions in the South African mines in the late nineteenth century, mineralogists have theorized, and with considerable unanimity, that diamonds were formed by the intense heat of volcanic action in the old crater ducts of the Cretaceous period when dinosaurs still roamed the land and the American Rockies were just beginning to push their way upward.

Violent explosions of vaporous gas blew the contents of the crater ducts up through the crust of the earth nearly to the surface (in some instances through the surface) and linked them to plutonic rock which had hardened from its original molten state. This rock in time became known as "kimberlite," named after Kimberley township in South Africa. Thus, kimberlite is the parent deposit of the diamond. Diamond miners have long called this deposit "blue ground" because of its color, and they called the ducts leading through the volcanic rock "pipes." The pipes are the source of the diamonds.

When the first diamond came into the hands of man, to be cut, polished, and displayed, can only be speculated about. The first known source was India and possibly as long ago as four thousand years, but this is conjecture. A little later the evidence becomes more concrete. The King James version of the Bible, the Book of Exo-

dus, relates that in the fourth month after the Lord deliv-
ered the Israelites from Egypt into the Sinai Desert (now
a disputed no-man's land of the wars between Israel and
Egypt) he called Moses to the mountaintop, gave him the
ten commandments and certain other instructions.
These included the making of vestments for Moses'
brother, Aaron, who was to serve as high priest, and
advised the inclusion of diamonds in the breastplate.
Since this account was written about six hundred years
after the occurrence, the language and nomenclature
may have changed.

In any event, by the fourth century B.C. India was well
known as a source for diamonds and was, in fact, the only
one for almost two thousand years thereafter. For many
centuries India's diamonds remained at home or in the
hands of travelers who carried them back to their own
homelands, largely as personal possessions. The writ-
ings of Pliny the Younger, Manilius, and others reveal
that the Greeks knew of diamonds in the first century
A.D., and there is evidence of diamond trading with
Rome before the fall of the Empire in 476 A.D. Actual
widespread trading, though, did not begin until about
the tenth century A.D. and even then was confined largely
to the Middle East until the Portuguese navigators
opened the Red Sea route to India and returned quantities of the stones to Europe.

There are a dozen different legends as to how the first
diamond was found in South Africa. Only certain is that
the finder was a child, perhaps black, perhaps white,
who, in either case, probably got a pat on the head as a

reward when the stone was turned over to the farm owner, Schalk van Neikerk. The farm was near the village of Hopetown in the northern part of the Cape Colony. The year was 1867. The Cape Colony was then a British colony. Its neighbors, the Orange Free State and the Transvaal, where diamonds were to be found later, were at that time independent and under the control of their Dutch (Afrikan) settlers. Today the three provinces, with a fourth, Natal, make up the country of South Africa.

Van Neikerk only suspected that the "pretty pebble" from the banks of the Orange River might be valuable and turned it over to a hunter-trader, John O'Reilly. O'Reilly took it to nearby Colesberg to the Civil Commissioner, who identified it as a diamond. This judgment was later confirmed by a mineralogist at Grahamstown. It weighed 21.25 carats and was subsequently purchased by Sir Philip Woodhouse, the British governor of the Cape Colony, for about $2,500. A few months later the stone was shown at the Paris World Exhibition. Later it was bought by De Beers as an historic relic and given the name of the Eureka, though in South Africa it is still known as the O'Reilly.

Two years later a black herder working for van Neikerk brought him another stone. Wiser this time, van Neikerk bought it from him, paying the astonishingly generous price of 500 sheep, eleven heifers, a horse, saddle, bridle, and gun, together worth some $2,000 and making the African possibly the richest black man in the Cape Colony. Van Neikerk handled this diamond himself. It turned out to be a perfect stone of 83.5 carats, was sold for $60,000, and became the Star of South Africa.

For a country which was in the economic doldrums at the time, South Africa took the news of the diamond finds between the Orange and the Vaal rivers with unexpected calmness, and it was not until 1870, when it was discovered that the stones were not confined to the rivers but existed as well in primary deposits in the area, that the real rush began. Some of the prospecting parties had fantastic luck and this did bring adventuring diamond seekers in by the hundreds.

Like the forty-niners of California a little earlier, they came in a dozen descriptions from a dozen nations. There were lawyers and bankers as well as tailors, barbers, clerks, carpenters, laborers, pastors—gamblers all. They came from the California fields, from Australia and South America, the slums of London and New York, from half the countries of the continent. There were women, too—wives, sisters, mothers, and even some virtually on their own. Within a few months after the big rush started there were 10,000 prospectors in the fields.

The site of the first deposit of diamonds—of "blue ground"—and the discovery that they were embedded in "pipes" came at the Jagersfontein farm in the Orange Free State in August of 1870. The second site came a month later with the discovery of the Dutoitspan deposits, the name taken from the farm owner, Abraham Paul Du Toit.

Deposits were found in the spring of 1871 on the Bultfontein farm, also in the Orange Free State, and soon thereafter on the farm of the brothers De Beers, a little over a mile away. A second digging was opened on the De Beers place soon thereafter. All of the discoveries resulted in mines that were to become famously rich and, through a series of circumstances the De Beers name later became the symbol of diamonds worldwide. The second De Beers mine was also known as the Colesberg Kopje (or hill) and in time was renamed the Kimberley. The name was also given to the city which grew up around it (actually four towns) with a total present population of nearly 100,000 people.

In those early days the mining methods were primitive, in many ways like the panning of gold by prospectors in any field. Claims were staked on the hills near the rivers. The gravel usually lay between boulders which had to be removed by sweat and muscles. The gravel and sand was then loaded into a cart. When full it was taken to the river to be washed in sieves of descending size mesh. The larger mesh screened out the big stones and any large diamonds among them. After the first sieving the gravel was worked through the smaller sieves until the load was all washed. Diamonds, while not really attractive (about like a small potato, it has been said) are easily spotted and, in those days, usually with "whoops and hollers."

Mining camps sprang up overnight around the diggings and, for all the vast cultural disparity of the miners, the deportment in the African fields was remarkably peaceable. The climate was dry and generally healthful, a blessing since most of the shelters were canvas. Doctors were virtually nonexistent, so the miners shared medical lore and ointments in treating each other's injuries and illnesses.

Several of the world's more famous diamonds were found in those early days. Two of the earliest were given the name of Victoria, after England's reigning monarch. One was found at the Jagersfontein diggings in 1884. It weighed 466 carats and was originally called the Imperial. Taken to Amsterdam, it was cut into several stones, the largest of which was 184.5 carats and renamed Victoria. The other was found in the De Beers mines in 1880 and appeared rather mysteriously in London where it was named, displayed, and then disappeared. The stone weighed, by various accounts, in the neighborhood of 250 carats. Both Victorias are rumored to have found their ways eventually to princes of India. The Jubilee was found at the Jagersfontein diggings in 1895 and cut into a 243.35-carat stone in 1897, the year of Queen Victoria's Diamond Jubilee (after which it was named).

Largest of the early finds was the Excelsior, also found at Jagersfontein. It weighed 995.2 carats and for several years was the largest diamond in the world. The crude stone, reportedly, was spotted by a black workman loading a truck in an open-pit digging, stowed away in his pocket, and then presented to the mine manager after work ceased. Today workers in the South African mines are rewarded generously for spotting stones in the mines where they work and the custom was followed even then. The finder was given a riding horse and saddle, plus some cash.

The peace of the diamond fields was not to remain

undisturbed for long. The fields lay on the western borders of the Orange Free State and the Transvaal. Neither
these borders nor the governments of the two states had
been clearly defined. Until the discovery of diamonds the
Dutch-descended Boers had clearly outnumbered the
British-descended in all of South Africa, but the sudden
surge of immigrants to the diamond fields changed all of
that, for the newcomers were predominently of the British Empire in origin.

The land where the diamonds were discovered was not
entirely worthless. Sheep grazed there, though it took a
number of acres to support one ewe and her lamb. But
the land was not considered very valuable either, and no
one had worried very much about where it lay or who
governed.

It was inevitable that in the course of time the miners
who were newly arrived and the Boers who had long
been settled there should clash. The Boers were conservative, staid, independent, and vastly contemptuous of
the restless, improvident lives of the miners. The Boers
wanted no part of the diamonds, or only a little, perhaps
—such as royalties—but mostly they just wanted these
brash invaders to get out so they could go back to being
isolated farmers who could go months without seeing a
stranger.

The British government, finally conscious of the fact
that diamonds were valuable and that there seemed to be
a lot of them out there, in 1871 heeded the urging of
Cecil Rhodes, head of the British South Africa Company,
and annexed both the Orange Free State and the Trans-

vaal, to "preserve order," they said. This quite naturally infuriated the Boers; and also, it set hard and firm the first step that led to the Boer War of 1899.

The two decades following the discovery of diamonds saw more modern techniques enter the diamond fields, the employment of black labor to increase the scope of operations, the proliferation of smuggling and illicit diamond buying, the establishment of compounds to prevent or at least stem this—and a titanic battle between two Englishmen for control of the diamond fields. One was Oxford-educated Cecil Rhodes, the Empire-oriented entrepreneur who dreamt of making the whole of Africa a British colony. The other was Barney Barnato, born Barnett Isaacs in the unwalled Jewish ghetto of White Chapel in East London. The Isaacs grandfather had set up a boxing ring in his basement and taught Barney and brother Harry that a pugnacious attack was the best defense and had kept them both in school until they were fourteen. They thus learned English as well as Hebrew, and could both read and write it.

Both boys were passionately attracted to the world of London vaudeville and taught themselves acrobatics as an entry. After mild success and with the money they had accumulated, Harry first and then Barney took off for the diamond fields.

Here the bright star which had hung over their careers still shone and they were successful in their early diamond mining efforts. They were also perspicacious enough to realize that surer profits lay in allied areas and, in 1874, set up the Barnato Brothers Brokerage firm. Then, two years or so later, Barney began a bold operation of buying up mining claims.

In the meantime Cecil Rhodes had also realized that as long as there were a thousand owners of the diamond mines it could not help remaining a wildly haphazard operation both in production and—more important, from Rhodes' point of view—in marketing the stones. So he, like Barnato, began buying up claims which, quite predictably, in the course of time put the two men on a collision course.

Barnato had formed the Barnato Diamond Mining Company in 1880 and Rhodes the De Beers Mining Company, named after the great mine developed on the land of two brothers, Johannes Nicholas and Diederick Arnoldus De Beers, which had been one of his earliest acquisitions. (The De Beers brothers also held shares.) Both Rhodes and Barnato acquired, in time, massive financial backing, including members of the international financiering Rothschild family.

The showdown came in 1888 and, after weeks of infighting and negotiations, the two companies were merged into the De Beers Consolidated Mines, with Cecil Rhodes firmly in charge. The price was high. Barnato, the White Chapel slum kid, emerged with a check for 5,338,650 British pounds and was made governor of the corporation for life with an undisclosed share in the organization—if little of the control. The check, adequately framed, hangs in the De Beers corporate offices today (it was cashed). Two members of the Rothschild family are on the present De Beers board of directors.

In the meantime, of course, gold had been discovered on the Witwatersrand River and Barnato turned from diamonds to another precious commodity. He organized Barnato Consolidated Mines and the Barnato bank. He was successful with gold as he had been with diamonds, but not in another area, the control of his health. On June 14, 1897, sick and bored with being constantly ill, he jumped off a ship bound for England.

From its original holdings De Beers expanded until it controlled almost every diamond digging in South Africa and in South West Africa, now Namibia. And also, of course, the company bought up most of the diamonds produced elsewhere, including eastern Brazil where diamonds had been discovered in the early 1700s.

Kimberley grew from an instant mining settlement of tents and shacks into the present graceful city which draws its strength from four great mines and from the De Beers company, which has its headquarters there in a two-story building with a wrought-iron balcony on Stockdale Street. Visitors to Kimberley can see the biggest man-made hole in the world, dug to extract more than fourteen million carats of diamonds before it was worked out in 1914. It covers almost forty acres and is about 1,300 feet deep, two-thirds of it filled with water. It is called, understandably, the Big Hole. There is a Kimberley Museum and tourists may visit the Bulfontein mine for a fee of thirty-five cents.

Between the De Beers takeover in 1888 and today, many famous diamonds have been taken from the mines in the Kimberley area. Greatest of these is the famous

Cullinan, the largest diamond in the rough ever found. The discoverer was the mine superintendent, Frederick Wells, who was making a routine inspection of the Premier mine near Pretoria when his eye caught a flash of brightness on the wall just above him. He extracted the stone he had seen, carried it to the surface, and it proved to be a raw diamond weighing 3,601 carats—or a little over twenty-one ounces—and measured 2 x 2½ x 4 inches or about the size of a woman's fist. It was named for Sir Thomas Cullinan, who had presided at ceremonies opening the mine and happened to be visiting the diggings that day.

The Jonker, all 726 carats of it, was found on the farm of Jacobus Jonker, also near Pretoria. It was, of course, sold to De Beers and thence to Harry Winston, the dean of the New York diamond dealers. Winston had it cut into several stones, including the 125.65-carat stone which retained the Jonker name. It was sold to King Farouk during his reign as ruler of Egypt and he in turn sold it to Queen Ratna of Nepal.

South Africa has no monopoly, of course, on famous diamonds. The Great Mogul of India, found in the seventeenth century, weighed 787.50 carats and, after cutting, came into the possession of Shah Jehan, who built the Taj Mahal for his favorite wife. Shah Jehan also owned the smaller but more famous Koh-i-noor, which was discovered much earlier, in 1804, and passed down to Jehan by a long line of Moguls. And there is, of course, the celebrated Hope diamond which made its first appearance with a London dealer in 1830 and was purchased by the gem collector, Henry Philip Hope. The Hope is small, compared to others less famous, but renowned for its great beauty—and also the bad luck it brought to its owners. It is now on permanent display at the Smithsonian Institution in Washington, D.C.

The largest, and most famous, of all diamonds found in Brazil was the 726.60-carat President Vargas, mined in the state of Minas Gerais. North America's most notable stone is the Uncle Sam, found in 1924 in Arkansas, which has the only diamond field in the United States. The raw stone weighed 40.23 carats and was shaped into a 14.42-carat emerald-cut stone. The Russians discovered Kimberley pipes holding diamonds in Siberia in 1954, and probably found some noteworthy stones there but, if so, they are Iron Curtain secrets.

Diamond is the hardest stone man has yet discovered on this planet, ranking ahead of corundum (parent of the ruby), topaz, and of quartz, which takes a number of forms and colors and ends up often as one of the semiprecious stones. The diamonds the customer sees in jewelry stores may come from any one of perhaps two thousand different classifications of rough stones, and their individual quality may vary greatly. Professionals rate the cut stones into four separate categories, known in the trade as the four "Cs." These are carat, color, clarity, and cut, and there are many different gradations of both color and clarity—scores of shades and pellucidity.

The price of diamonds has risen tremendously in the past quarter of a century, far surpassing even the usual

inflation rate, largely due to an increased demand and a
controlled supply. The girl who is promising her hand
no longer is content to grace it with a quarter-carat diamond but wants that size doubled or more. Also, while
the diamond was once popular only with the wealthy of
many nations, now the engagement stone, commonplace
in the United States, has become more universal. People
of Europe and the Middle East have always hoarded the
diamond as an ace in the hole against political emergen-
cies. Now people with extra money in any country may
be using the diamond as an investment or a hedge
against inflation and something to enjoy at the same
time.

This latter may have a question mark going with it.
Elizabeth Taylor must pay about $60,000 a year insur-
ance on her million-dollar-plus necklace and even then
she is permitted to take it out of the vault and appear
with it in public only thirty times a year—which comes
out to about $2,000 a wearing.

The controlled supply system, of course, has been
built up over three-quarters of a century and is now in
the most capable hands of Harry Oppenheimer, Chairman of the Board of De Beers Consolidated Mines, Ltd.
By either mining or buying up most of the rough stones
mined in the world, De Beers—with ample cash reserves
—can release or withhold stones to the market according
to the demand, and thus effectively destroy any chance
of wild price fluctuation.

(Harry Oppenheimer is the son of Sir Ernest Oppenheimer, who became chairman of the company in 1929

and bought up diamonds during the Depression to hold the price line. Harry Oppenheimer is also chairman of the Anglo-American Corporation of South Africa, which has many interlocking ties to De Beers. Anglo-American is a conglomerate with vast interests, largely mineral.)

De Beers sells to diamond brokers through a subsidiary called, aptly, the Central Selling Organization, with headquarters at Number 2 Charterhouse Street in the heart of London's diamond market, near St. Paul's Cathedral. The nine-story building now housing the organization replaced a more modest structure on the same site which caught an incendiary bomb during World War II.

Sales are conducted there as often as every three weeks or as seldom as every three months, depending again on supply and demand, and the brokers arrive by invitation only.

Customers of Central Selling number about three hundred and they are queried two weeks in advance of one of the regular "sights" as to their approximate needs, and they are then issued invitations which let them into the building. If there are 294 buyers, there are 294 packets made up. Each is allocated to one buyer according to his requests—and to De Beers' very accurate estimates of his needs at that particular time and in his particular territory.

The buyer arrives and receives his packet. He may, if he wishes, take it to a long table before tall windows and in the good north light inspect his allotment (which is why the sales are called "sights"). The packets vary considerably—perhaps from $100,000 up to eight or ten million, depending on the size of the business the buyer maintains. After inspecting his packet, the diamond dealer may discuss the stones with De Beers' selling officials, if he has the temerity. This is rarely done, for the buyer must take all the stones or none, and there is no picking and choosing, no mixing of contents. The broker, of course, does not have to accept his packet, though if he doesn't it is quite likely he will not be invited back for some time, maybe never.

Many buyers don't look at their stones at Number 2 Charterhouse Street, simply accepting what they get on blind faith. Some may never look. They just raise the price on the envelope by some percentage and sell it to another dealer who is not on the invitation list. Payment to De Beers, incidentally, is made on acceptance of the packet—or within a few hours.

After leaving Number 2 Charterhouse Street most of the diamonds are cut and then make their way to one of the sixteen Diamond Clubs which comprise the World Federation of the Diamond Bourses. The Federation has headquarters in Amsterdam, long the center of world diamond cutting and dealing.

The diamond clubs are another world to themselves. New York has two, the largest of which is at 30 West 47th Street, where, according to an exhaustively researched account in *Forbes* magazine, 90 percent of this nation's diamonds pass in business deals. The area is a tight cluster of large and small offices housing more than a thousand dealers, cutters, and setters, with an equal number in allied pursuits—insurers, appraisers, and legal specialists.

Small operators may work on the sidewalk but the bigger dealers are in the tall surrounding buildings, well protected by a wealth of security measures. The memberships of all sixteen diamond clubs is close to ten thousand persons. The New York club on 47th Street has a membership of about 1,500 and it is in the club building itself that most of the diamond deals take place. Here, as at Number 2 Charterhouse Street, the sellers display their stones on long tables before north windows and bargain in quiet tones with those who have come to buy. Most of the members know each other, many are related, and the deals are on faith.

Memberships in the diamond clubs are difficult to achieve, requiring multiple sponsorship, close inspection, and impeccable financial records. Membership in one means membership in all. Once the haggling over one stone or twenty is over, and the buyer and seller have agreed to terms, they shake hands. The seller then wishes the buyer "mazel and broche," the Hebraic term for "good luck and blessings," and the deal is complete. The phrase is used by both Jewish and non-Jewish merchants and is considered the linchpin of whatever arrangements have been made.

Rules of the diamond clubs are strict and the penalty for transgression severe. Controversies may be taken to the club's Board of Arbitrators for decisions and these are normally accepted. They may be appealed to the Board of Directors, but rarely are and even more rarely do they appear in court. Any member who fails to abide by a ruling is stripped of his membership and barred from the club. Notice immediately goes to Amsterdam, which in turn notifies all other clubs and their doors are closed henceforth to the disbarred one. He is, in effect, banned from the big-time diamond business.

Diamonds are De Beers and De Beers is South Africa. All three are inseparably linked. De Beers and diamonds contribute a sizeable chunk to South Africa's gross national product, tax fund, better-paid labor force and—by no means least—prestige, and will probably continue to do so under whatever form of government may evolve there. The diamond is in itself a superlative: a commodity of beauty, esteem, and solidity. As De Beers says in a thousand display ads, "A Diamond Is Forever."

CHAPTER 4

The Gold

GOLD HAS BEEN found in Southern Africa for centuries, from traces to veins of almost pure ore. It was the basis of the wealth which built the famous walled city of Zimbabwe in the sixteenth century. Zimbabwe is now part of Rhodesia and the gold mines are no longer of major importance there; they were, in fact, far surpassed by the gold which was discovered in South Africa in 1887 and thereafter.

The discovery of the first gold reef, or vein, was made by an itinerant, one George Harrison, who was digging building stones on a farm near the Witwatersrand River. The site became known immediately as the Witwatersrand Reef. Harrison had been in the gold fields of Australia and knew gold-bearing quartz when he saw it. Digging further into his bed of stones, he was able to tell that he had dug into a shallow reef, or layer or vein, of ore that almost certainly was worth mining.

The Boers of the Transvaal, where the discovery was

made, wanted an influx of gold prospectors no more than they had wanted the earlier diamond seekers, and at the first hint of gold they passed laws prohibiting the disclosure of the locations of any minerals there.

Man has not yet devised the law which could keep the discovery of gold a secret. Within a few weeks the rush to the Witwatersrand was in full flow. Harrison staked out a claim, sold it for thirty dollars, and wandered on his peripatetic way. According to one report, he was eaten by a lion somewhat to the east in the Transvaal.

Gold was formed on earth probably about four or five trillion years ago, along with iron, copper, and other metals, at a time when the earth's only living things were a few elementary forms of marine life, algae, and perhaps worms.

Man, who arrived considerably later, two to three million years ago, was laggard in discovering any metals— bronze about 5000 B.C. and iron a couple of thousand years later. Gold he probably came across at some time between the two periods. It has been found in the form of ornaments in tombs almost five thousand years old, still bright, still untarnished. The gold mask of Egypt's Tut-ankh-amen shone brilliantly when the Earl of Carnarvon opened the tomb some 3,250 years after the famous king's burial.

The allure of gold has been called absurd ("Why go to the ends of the world to dig up gold just to bury it again in a hole at Fort Knox?"), ludicrous, and barbaric. Never mind. Gold has been the most treasured metal in the world for ages and remains so today. No other property in the earth or on it approaches gold in universal appeal. There is no single reason for this, rather a combination of many. Gold is virtually indestructible. Most of the gold ever mined is still around in some form or other. It does not tarnish or corrode. Nitric is the only acid to affect it. Coins from a galleon sunk two hundred years before look new and bright. The ancient city of Troy's golden treasures were unearthed untarnished.

Gold is rare. In the last five hundred years, since the start of record-keeping, all of the gold mined in the world would make a very heavy cube only fifty feet in all dimensions—about the size of a three-story building occupying only a sixth of an average city block.

Gold is a soft metal, nearly as soft as lead, and so malleable that an ounce of it—cold—can be hammered into a thin (as thin as five millionths of an inch), translucent film 108 feet square. That same ounce can be drawn into a very fine wire fifty miles long. Next to silver, gold is the world's finest conductor of electricity and can be printed on plastic strips for computers and other devices, one strip replacing miles of wiring. A gold bridge made by a dentist will last a lifetime. Gold has been selected by craftsmen for thousands of years for use in every form of art, including ancient objects of pagan worship.

With all of the foregoing, gold's chief allure always has been its beauty and the almost mythical appeal which accompanies it. It adorns thrones, temples, and altars, royal and priestly robes and other apparel, draperies and tapestries. It decorates great buildings and complements expensive books. The golden wedding band has long been a symbol of fidelity in marriage. And, as jewelry, it adorns men and women of all ages and races. Diamonds may be a girl's best friend, but it has been remarked that few of them will turn down a gold bracelet when offered.

The continent of Africa has been associated with gold for thousands of years. The earliest known date in history was the adoption of the Egyptian calendar in 4241 B.C. and it was just eight hundred years later, about 3400 B.C. that King Menes, who united what had formerly been the kindoms of Upper and Lower Egypt, wrote about the value of gold which arrived from the Upper Nile. References are to be found of hard-rock mining in Egypt as early as the fourteenth century B.C.

History credits the Lydian government of King Alyattes with devising the first coinage system, in the sixth century B.C. This early money was formed by stamping a piece of metal—copper, silver, or gold—with the royal monogram. If the credit rating of the government was good it could even place an evaluation on the coin higher than its actual weight value and it would be accepted universally in the trading world of that day.

The Greeks, and later the Romans, certainly knew gold in quantity. Pre-Islamic Arabs bartered for it on Africa's East Coast and probably ventured farther south, possibly to the Rhodesian mines, as early as the seventh or eighth century A.D. Certainly they were there just a few hundred years later.

The gold which Spain extracted from Central and South America at sword point made her a dominant world power in the sixteenth and the seventeenth centuries while, for many of those years, the Portuguese were searching for the lost mines of Solomon and adding to their store of gold mostly by barter with the metal merchants of India. Gold was found in Russia in 1744 but created little stir.

Then the great California gold rush began in 1848–49, followed almost immediately thereafter by the discovery of the yellow metal in Australia. Both of these highly publicized and dramatized finds stimulated the enthusiasm which greeted the discovery on the Witwatersrand and added greatly to the wild rush to get to the new diggings.

The early prospectors at the new discovery site went immediately to the nearest river, creek, or stream to try their luck with the tried-and-true method of panning. Anyone could do it then; anyone can now.

It requires a pan, basin, bowl—almost any size or shape, though a shallow metal vessel probably works best. With this in hand the prospector then scoops up a double handful, say, of loose dirt and gravel, places it in the pan and fills the pan with water.

Since gold is almost twenty times as heavy as water and several times heavier than the dirt or gravel surrounding it, the gold will sink to the bottom of the pan. The prospector goes through a normal, easily imitated process, shaking the pan vigorously, lifting out bigger stones, shaking again, tipping the pan to let water and loose dirt flow out, repeating the procedure until the grains of gold (if any) lie alone and gleaming in the bottom of the pan.

When panning didn't work, the miners tried the pick and shovel, looking for nuggets which weren't there. They even improvised crude rock-crushers as a last and futile resort of individual enterprise.

What George Harrison had discovered, and what was almost immediately found to be characteristic of South African gold, was layers or reefs of rock interlarded with the metal. Crushed and processed, a ton or so of the ore-bearing rock would produce an ounce or so of gold. It was a highly profitable operation but it required organization, machinery, and capital. These pioneers faced a discouraging situation. The individual mining picture looked bleak, and the Transvaal, as a place to live, was not precisely hospitable either.

The Kalahari Desert, the Drakensberg mountain range east and west, and the Vaal and Limpopo rivers, on the south and north, form a rough square of land somewhat larger than 100,000 square miles. Now part of South Africa, it is a land of cities, roads, rail lines, and gold mines, though still untamed in places. In 1887 it had a wild animal population that would make any zoo envious —rhinoceros, zebras, springbok, ostriches, lions, leopards, hyenas, and jackals. The land contained perhaps 2,500 white people and more than a quarter million black Africans of a score of tribes, who had been pushed around by the white Boers for half a century. On a chance encounter they might be friendly or they might not. Certainly the lions and the leopards weren't.

The Boer farmers lived either in the wagons in which they may have made their original journey to the area, or in just about the same kind of mud huts the native blacks built, for there was no lumber and building stones were findable only in certain spots and then not easily. The roads were trails between villages of from four or five houses to as many as a hundred—settlements like Potchefstroom and Rustenburg. The Transvaal parliament sometimes met in one of the latter two.

The Boers, according to their own laws (altered by a later British-dominated government) were entitled to six thousand acres each—give or take a few hundred, for there were no real boundaries or surveys or even decent maps. The land was used mostly for grazing cattle, sheep, and goats, and the farmers were devoted destroyers of the game which needed to share the pasturage and of the predators which menaced the livestock.

The early miners found these Dutch-descended Boers not much friendlier than some of the African blacks. The Boers hadn't come to this remote, uncivilized, and hostile land because they liked crowds. They were a fiercely independent, Calvinistically-moral people who didn't want to be fenced in and who knew quite well that the superiority of the white man over the rest of humanity was a thing that God himself had ordained.

On the heels of the early rugged prospectors came the men who had been successful in the diamond fields, men like Cecil Rhodes and Barney Barnato and others less well known. They brought in engineers and mineralogists, machinery and—most important—millions of dollars in capital. They bought up claims and began an immediate power struggle. The early miners went to work for them—or went home.

Even in the latter part of the nineteenth century developing a mine on the Witwatersrand Reef in South Africa was a project involving hundreds of thousands of dollars. And, as men went deeper into the earth for gold, the cost increased. Today, like the cost of a loaf of bread, the early figures have gone up, way up. Below are data from the South African Chamber of Mines:

$37,500,000	Shaft sinking
13,500,000	Reduction plant
10,500,000	Underground development
2,625,000	Compressed air
3,750,000	Electricity
1,125,000	Ventilation
1,500,000	Water pumping
3,000,000	Other underground equipment
2,625,000	Surface buildings
375,000	Surface transport and services
12,750,000	Houses, hotels, etc.
750,000	Miscellaneous expenses
$90,000,000	Total

The procedures of sinking one deep-level mine in the Far West Rand gold field recently is indicative of why the cost is so enormous. In this case, the original mining lease covered some ten thousand acres. Bore holes were drilled as the first step. An analysis of the earth and rock brought to the surface in this case indicated that the field would produce maybe a billion and a half dollars worth of gold. (They might just as easily have indicated no gold at all.)

Men then began the round-the-clock job of sinking

two shafts to a final depth of 6,700 feet—more than a mile beneath the surface. The work shaft was 31½ feet in diameter and the ventilation shaft 24 feet. They were 280 feet apart.

For this purpose a multideck stage was suspended over the shafts to provide a movable-platform work area. Workmen in the shafts drilled holes, inserted explosive charges, were hoisted to the surface, the blasts detonated, the debris cleared, and the process repeated. The inside of the shaft was lined with concrete.

It sounds simple, but of course isn't. Exploratory work may take months and months. Once committed, the shaft-sinking work is done with a dedicated intensity because it is essential to get maximum usage out of the millions of dollars worth of equipment being used.

When the shafts are completed, "stopes" are dug; that is, horizontal tunnels from the vertical shaft, and from these the mining is done. When in full production about 12,000 men will take the drop down the mine every day, six days a week. From their eight hours of labor each day, the hoists will bring up about 10,000 tons of waste and gold.

Today in South Africa there are fifty-odd mines being worked in seven major fields: Central Rand, East Rand, West Rand, and Far West Rand, all near Johannesburg and the site of the original gold discovery, Klerksdorp to the southwest, Evander to the southeast, and the Orange Free State field, usually referred to as the OFS mines. (Gold is mined elsewhere in Southern Africa, principally Rhodesia, but the fields of this one country, South

Africa, are so much richer they tend to overshadow the rest.)

These mines are controlled by eight major companies of which the Anglo-American Corporation of South Africa, Ltd., is the richest, largest, and most compelling. Anglo-American is the parent company of thirteen of the fifty-one mines which produce some 40 percent of all South African gold. Anglo-American is closely linked to De Beers and diamonds, both financially and by corporate management. Its headquarters is in Johannesburg, at 44 Main Street, where it dominates the city's business district. Chairman of both De Beers and Anglo-American is Harry Oppenheimer, as his father was before him.

The story of the Oppenheimers is really the story of De Beers and Anglo-American. The companies are inseparable from each other and also from the Oppenheimers.

The elder member of the family, Ernest, was born in Germany, served an apprenticeship for a London diamond firm which sent him to South Africa and the mining scene in 1903 at the ripe old age of twenty-six. Not long after his arrival a new diamond mine opened, the Premier. De Beers found it uninteresting, but Oppenheimer thought otherwise and persuaded his firm to invest several million dollars.

The Premier proved to be enormously successful (the world's largest diamond, the Cullinan, was found there later) and this, and other successful Oppenheimer operations, led to the incorporation of Anglo-American in 1917. The new company and Oppenheimer found the move to the gold fields quite natural, opened up the East and West Rand mines, among others, and the alluvial beach deposits along the coast in Namibia. Then Oppenheimer moved in on De Beers, through management tactics and by buying up big blocks of stock on the open market. By 1926 he was on the board of directors and three years later had powered his way to the chairmanship. By this time he had been knighted by a grateful George V of England, South Africa still being a part of the Empire.

During the Depression, Sir Ernest, with all the financial backing he could muster from both companies, bought up and held diamonds—South Africa's and the gem stones of other mines in other lands as well—parceling them out in small lots to preserve prices.

When the market lifted its head during the late thirties and diamonds again were in demand, Sir Ernest was free to move into other fields—copper, coal, uranium, iron and steel, even breweries and motor cars, until Anglo-American became one of the giant conglomerates of the world. And when Sir Ernest moved on he left both corporations in the hands of his son, Harry Oppenheimer, who displayed his father's talent for organization, management, and expansion.

Gold has been everybody's favorite commodity for thousands of years and its value, while varying greatly during the centuries, has never been negligible or doubted. Over the ages of civilization many objects have been used as a medium of exchange, from cattle to shells to dried fish. Hammurabi, the great king of ancient Baby-

Ionia, began the use of silver, and nations have been using minted coins—often gold—much of the time since. Some three hundred years ago nations began printing paper money which, up until World War I, was usually tied to gold reserves. When this became impractical the value of money was related to another currency which was backed by gold, often—at that time—the United States dollar, which was on a full gold standard from 1900 until 1933. At that time—the Great Depression— the United States shifted to a modified gold standard, ceased the use of gold coins, prohibited private owner- ship of bulk gold, and maintained the price by paying $35 an ounce for any offered. Tons of it were stored in the vaults of Fort Knox.

Then in 1968 the American government adopted a policy of letting the price of gold float, find its own level. It hovered around the $35 mark for a couple of years and then began to climb. By December 1, 1974, when the United States government began permitting its citizens to own gold like the rest of the world, the price had climbed about 500 percent to around $175 an ounce. It has been holding fairly steady since, at about $150 to $160 an ounce.

When the law on the private possession of gold was relaxed, it was widely predicted that there would be an immediate rush to banks and dealers by private citizens to buy gold—for speculation, hoarding, or maybe just plain fun; that specialty stores and expensive boutiques would have small gold bars neatly packaged or gift- wrapped, all ready for the customers.

It didn't happen. There was no rush, possibly because people realized that the great leap from $35 an ounce to the present price wouldn't be likely to happen again. And, if there were people who wanted bulk gold to store in safe deposit boxes or bury in the backyard, they got it quietly at the bank. A gold bar, after all, is not something you want to display on the mantle.

The effect of the great price increase of gold on the mining industry of Southern Africa, of course, was simply to increase the total value of the product and the national income. In South Africa gold exports in 1972 gave the government its first favorable balance of trade.

CHAPTER 5

South Africa

S OUTH AFRICA is a country lavishly endowed by nature with spectacular beauty, a magnificent climate, and a munificent treasure chest of mineral wealth. Jan Christiaan Smuts, twice Prime Minister, said that when God created the world He finished with a handful of precious materials left over—"not only gold and diamonds and other minerals, but beauty and something to appeal to the human spirit"—and scattered them across South Africa.

It is also a country where a minority of white people, about one-sixth of 23 million all told, have perpetuated total control with racial policies which are abhorrent to most of the rest of the world. The Right Reverend Joost de Blank, former Archbishop of Cape Town and himself (like Smuts) an Afrikaner, has excoriated the South African apartheid policies as "anti-Christian, inhuman, and . . . suicidal."

The Cape of Good Hope, which is to South Africa as

Plymouth Rock is to America, was discovered in 1488 by the pupils of Portugal's Prince Henry the Navigator, but they were intent on opening a route to India and it was not until more than 150 years later that the white man landed there to remain. In April of 1652 three small ships commissioned by the Dutch East India Company and under the command of Jan van Riebeeck dropped anchor in the excellent natural harbor to establish a "refreshment station," calling their settlement Capetown (now Cape Town).

In addition to their normal ship's complement, the three vessels carried about eighty men, along with a dozen women and children. They were left at Capetown with food for several months, plus tools for building, seeds for planting, and guns for hunting, or protection, if needed.

Holland at this point in history was free of the crushing Spanish rule which had oppressed the nation for three-quarters of a century, and had become one of Europe's leading powers. The Dutch East India Company, an amalgamation of what had been a score of smaller companies, sent adventuring sea captains throughout the East and they brought home the wealth of the Indies.

The voyage from India to the homeland, however, was too long to make without a stop for "refreshments"—in the literal sense of the word, fresh meat, fresh water, and most particularly, fresh vegetables and fruit to prevent scurvy. Hence, the Capetown settlement. Its mission was to plant and hunt, not to explore or to found a traditional colony.

The Dutch found the Capetown area already sparsely inhabited by the Khoi-Khoi tribes, small black natives they called "Hottentots" and whom they immediately began to take advantage of, usurping their lands and expropriating their cattle with a value and payment they, themselves, set. In time, quite naturally, the Khoi-Khoi resented such treatment and went to war. Their spears and poisoned arrows were not a good match for the flintlocks of the Dutch, however, and they eventually either submitted or withdrew farther inland.

This mini-war was in 1657, only five years after the first arrival, and at about the same time two other events took place which set the pattern for the next two hundred years.

The Dutch East India Company was, at this time, a government-chartered power-structure with its own army and navy, its own laws, courts, and judges. It made treaties, established (and overturned) governments, and controlled tracts of land larger then many nations. So it was with scarcely a thought that the company granted nine employees (who had finished their contracted time in Capetown) tracts of land in the Cape Colony and gave them the right of settlement as "free burghers." The company also permitted them, and other Capetowners, to purchase slaves who were brought in from Java, the Indonesian island also ruled by the Dutch East India Company, and from Madagascar, off the southeast African coast.

With the advent of slavery, the stratification of the local society also began, with all the intolerance and prejudices of racial attitudes. More settlers from the Capetown settlement followed the original nine and these were augmented by Huguenot refugees fleeing another form of bigotry, this one religious, promulgated by France's Louis XIV. These settlers, finding the soil mostly too shallow for profitable farming for long, turned to cattle raising, acquiring tracts of land in 6,000-acre chunks either by grant or purchase at a very low price. In order to achieve this they pushed farther and farther inland, dispossessing the Khoi-Khoi and the San (Bushman) tribes, who often found themselves with a choice of becoming either impressed labor or of starving.

Had the newly-become Afrikaners followed the pattern of Australia and Canada—that is, brought in white labor from Europe—the slave and master situation would not have developed, or not to the same degree. But, with every white man having either (or both) slave labor or impressed labor—and there was very little difference—there developed rapidly and naturally the concept of white man's work and black man's labor. And every white man, regardless of education or culture, became a "gentleman" in the parlance of the day. Many of them, by the late eighteenth century, had come to regard distinctions in color as divinely ordained and socially absolute. And with each generation the white settlers took more and more land from tribes which had occupied it before and either absorbed them as labor or drove them farther and farther inland.

Holland continued to be the ruling force in the south-

ern tip of Africa until 1794 when a French Revolutionary
army invaded Holland for a second time, transformed it
into the Batavian Republic, and made it a reluctant ally.
The British, as part of the coalition fighting the French,
recognized the value of protecting the route to India and
sent a peaceful occupying force into Table Bay Harbor
at Capetown. It remained for seven years with full local
acquiescence, withdrew for two years after the Treaty of
Amiens, and then went back in 1806, this time to stay. Its
permanent occupation was legalized at the 1814 Treaty
of Paris after Napoleon's first abdication.

In the early part of the nineteenth century, when the
British took over the southern tip of Africa, she considered its value much as had the Dutch East India Company—as a way-stop and a strong point on the sea route
to India. In fact, the colony was regarded as pretty much
of a nuisance until the discovery of diamond deposits in
1870 and the discovery of gold about sixteen years later.
That changed everything. But by virtue of the Treaty of
Paris, Britain in 1814 was acquiring an accumulation of
about 25,000 white Europeans, some 30,000 black
slaves, and an assortment of 20,000 Khoi-Khoi and San
blacks, Indians, and those people of mixed blood whom
the whites called "colored" and still do. The area was
unnamed, unbounded, and virtually ungoverned.

Actually, what later was to become the Union of South
Africa, and then the Republic of South Africa or just
South Africa, is a very personable creation of Mother
Nature. It lies almost entirely within the southern tem-
perate zone. In general appearance it is a shallow bowl,

with a sharp clifflike escarpment which rises steeply on the south and southeast. The interior—indeed, most of South Africa—is a vast plateau with an average elevation of 4,000 feet and rims which warp upward into the escarpment. Circling the plateau is a narrow coastal belt. The High Veld of the plateau has a generally monotonous surface—grassy undulations varied by vast flat plains, sometimes broken by *kopjes,* the small rock formations rising from the veld.

Much of the plateau is drained by the Orange River system with its two major tributaries, the Vaal and the Caledon. Total area of South Africa is just under 472,000 square miles, about twice the size of Texas. It has three capitals: administrative, Pretoria, population 570,000; legislative, Cape Town, population 1,100,000; and judicial, Bloemfontein, population 180,000. The best known of its urban centers is Johannesburg, with 1,500,000 people, and there is Durban on the Indian Ocean coast with 725,000 people.

According to the latest census, there are 23 million people in South Africa: whites, 3,751,328; colored, 2,018,453; Africans, 15,057,952; and Asians, 620,436.

Of the whites in South Africa, the Afrikaners make up roughly 60 percent. They are the people of Dutch descent who speak the Afrikaans language, an offshoot of Dutch. The English-speaking (no better term being available) make up the remaining 40 percent. The Afrikaners control the country politically.

The 15 million blacks are comprised of nine major peoples, each with its own language and, to some extent, its own culture, traditions, and customs. The following are government figures concerning each of the nine, with population and area of residence:

Xhosas, 4 million, living in Transkei and Ciskei
Zulu nation, 4 million, living in KwaZulu
Tswana, 2 million, living in Bophuthatswana
Northern Sotho, 2 million, living in Lebowa
Shangaan-Tsonga, 800,000, living in Gazankulu
Southern Sotho, 1.6 million, living in
   Basotho-QwaQwa
Vhavenda, 450,000, living in Venda
Swazi, 600,000, scattered
Ndebele, 400, scattered

The "coloreds" are mostly the descendants of the indigenous tribes of the Cape of Good Hope and the earliest European settlers in the area. (One historian notes: "The colored segment of the South African population began nine months after Jan van Riebeeck weighed anchor in the Capetown Harbor.") They live predominantly in the Cape Town area and the large urban centers, and most of them speak Afrikaans as their first language.

The first Indians arrived at Durban in 1860 in response to the cane growers' need for field laborers, the indigenous blacks having shown no aptitude nor inclination for the task. The Indians were indentured, first for three years and later for five, but many of them brought with them relatives and friends who came as free souls.

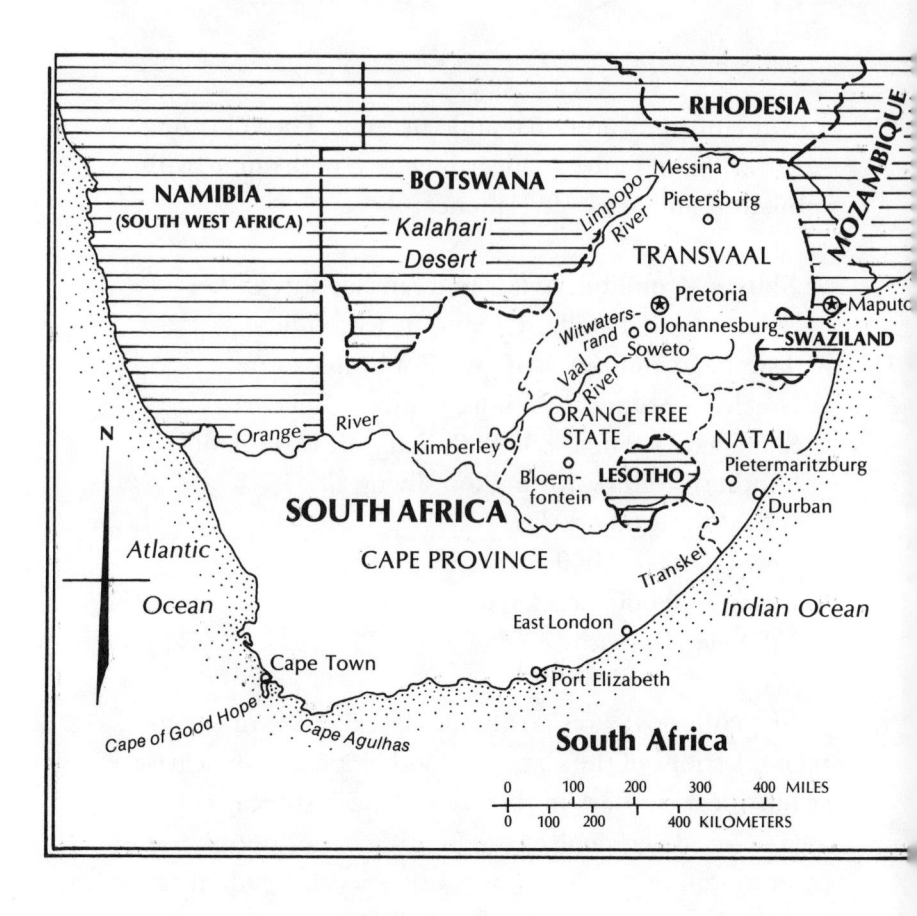

South Africa

| | 0 | 100 | 200 | 300 | 400 | MILES |
| 0 | 100 | 200 | | 400 | KILOMETERS |

And others were able to work or pay for their own passage. All came to escape the extreme poverty of India and found South Africa, bad as it could be, better than the land they had left.

At the end of their contracts the Indians had a choice of renewing their original indenture, returning to India at the government's expense, or accepting a plot of Crown land in lieu of passage. Most accepted the land.

Their presence in South Africa as permanent residents

eventually proved an embarrassment to the color-conscious whites. Contrary to the expectations of the whites, the Indians were not assimilated by either the blacks or the coloreds and chose instead to retain their own cultures and religions. The political situation which resulted provided, among other things, a training ground for Mahatma Gandhi, who worked for racial tolerance and justice in South Africa before taking up the same causes in India. The South African government finally, in 1961, came around to recognizing that the Indians had a right to remain and were, in the government's words, a "permanent responsibility" of South Africa. Today something less than 4 percent of the Indians are farm laborers. The majority are owners of truck farms or sugar plantations, are merchants or middle-class employees. They have maintained their Hindu and Moslem faiths, built beautiful temples and mosques, and have essentially retained their Eastern culture.

The word "boer" in the Dutch language means "farmer," and *boer* became the name applied generally to the Dutch immigrants who took up the land. (Later it became a proper noun and was often applied to all Dutch immigrants.) In their drive for new fertile lands for farming and grazing, the Boers and their sons pushed farther and farther inland. And in so doing they acquired the name of *trekboers,* literally, "farmers on the move." At first they encountered the blacks they called Hottentots (whom they virtually exterminated as "pests"), but as they forged farther into the interior they ran afoul of the Bantu, who were moving southward to escape the slave hunters and also in search of new lands.

The Bantu were a "nation" of blacks of two hundred or more tribes, languages, and culture, roughly allied and far advanced over either the Hottentots or Bushmen. The latter were still in the Stone Age; the Bantu had long known iron and other metals. The *trekboers* and the Bantu met head-on and the clash was violent, resulting in the "Kaffir Wars" which were fought intermittently for a hundred years, with charges and countercharges on both sides—of barbaric cruelty, the slaughtering of women and children, and endless aggression. In the long run the result was, however, inevitable: the Bantu were slain, conquered, and put to work or driven farther and farther back north.

When the British arrived to stay in 1814, and for a number of years thereafter, the land was under the old laws, or perhaps they were simply Dutch East India Company dictates which had endured since the first Boers began their pushes inland. The dispossessed black native must labor for the whites. It was virtually impossible for him to leave the farm he was bound to and his children were "apprenticed" to his employer.

Under the insistent prodding of Church of England missionaries, the British government first liberated the slaves—in 1834—and then passed new laws which gave legal rights to the blacks and the coloreds. And, on top of all this the British imported some 5,000 immigrants from their own country, settling them in the country above and inland from Port Elizabeth on the Indian Ocean coast.

All in all, this was a bit much for the exasperated Dutch. A johnny-come-lately and alien government had freed their slaves with what the Dutch called grossly inadequate compensation. The same new government had brought in a great chunk of English-speaking immigrants, altering to an unpleasant degree the white makeup of the country. And the new liberal laws, giving the blacks something like equal rights under the law and denying the Boers new lands when and where they wished to take them, were simply intolerable. So, they packed their belongings into covered wagons, hitched them to several span of oxen, corralled the rest of the livestock, chose leaders and companions, and took off to new lands.

Thus began the "Great Trek," the most significant event in Boer history, celebrated today in an annual fete with the men and women, dressed in the costume of that day, re-enacting parts of the historical journeys.

There were several expeditions under several leaders, guiding many hundred families and wagons. It was indicative, perhaps, of the Boer character that the same fiercely independent spirit which led them into the trek in the first place also prevented the leaders from getting along with each other and agreeing on one destination and presenting a unified front to the very real perils of the almost unknown land they were heading for. They quarrelled incessantly.

Leaders Louis Trigardt and Janse van Rensburg, in 1835 started with probably no more than thirty families, with a wagon or two apiece and their livestock. They moved from a point very near the Cape coast to the Transvaal where the leaders quarrelled. Van Rensburg and his party continued eastward and were lost without trace. Trigardt led his party on an incredibly difficult journey over the Drakensberg Range to what is now Lourenço Marques on the East Coast and thence by sea to Natal where only a few survivors arrived after a journey of three years.

Leader Hendrik Potgieter, with a much larger party, crossed what is now the Orange Free State, battled the very hostile Matabele tribe at Vegtop (Battle Hill), where they fought from the standard wagon train circle (much as the American pioneers were doing about the same time), lost all their livestock but eventually gathered with some 1,500 other *trekers* near today's Bloemfontein.

Leader Piet Retief and his followers, with nearly 1,000 wagons, had been part of the group with Potgieter until they, too, quarrelled and Retief took his party and headed for Natal on the Indian Ocean coast. On the coastal side of the Drakensberg the party ran into a wily Zulu chieftain who entrapped and slaughtered about half of them, including Retief. Undaunted, the remainder organized a small state near Natal, were reinforced by another group led by Andries Pretorius (after whom the city of Pretoria was named later) and retaliated against the Zulus by ensnaring them in turn in the Battle of Blood River in which 3,000 Zulus were killed. The Boers suffered only a few minor hurts.

In the years immediately following the Boers' migration from the Cape, the British wavered between a policy

of annexing the new settlements for their own protection
or letting them fight it out on their own with the native
blacks. The Boers who had reached Natal found the British already there. They tried unsuccessfully to oust them
and then left almost immediately northward where they,
with the other *trekers,* in time organized the South African Republic.

It was better known as two individual Dutch-governed
states, the Transvaal and the Orange Free State, the first
formed in 1852 and the second two years later. The
British in the Cape Colony and the Dutch in the Transvaal and the Orange Free State maintained an uneasy
relationship until the discovery of the first diamond in
1867 and then the discovery of gold in 1884–1886.

As Tom Hopkinson notes in his book *South Africa* for
the Life World Library, this discovery brought a tremendous impetus to "the British desire for prosperity and
orderliness" in the South Africa area. The two discoveries brought on the Boer War and, with a lavish abun-
dance of other minerals, are responsible for South
Africa's prosperity today.

Shortly after the discovery of diamonds there emerged
on the Southern African scene two figures, one British
and one Dutch, as different, to use an Afrikaner expres-
sion, as chalk and cheese, but strangely akin in the pas-
sionate determination of their poles-apart beliefs. They
were the English Cecil Rhodes and the Dutch Paul
Kruger, and they became, in the natural course of events,
bitter political and personal enemies.

Stephanus Johannes Paulus Kruger, usually known as

Paul or Oom Paul (Uncle Paul) Kruger, was born in the Cape Province in 1825. He made the Great Trek at the age of ten and, like all of his family, was a farmer. And, like all other able-bodied Boers, he served in the militia —in his case so successfully that he rose to be commanding general of the Transvaal organization.

In his early years Kruger was converted to the Afrikaner Calvinist faith. He took the French reformer's words literally and seriously, to the point that he regarded singing, even of religious songs, a sin unless it was done in strict privacy—preferably a hundred miles out on the veld. He was a dour man, regarded as virtually cheerless, but also as fair, honest, and able to see the opposing point of view.

In politics he was unbending in his determination to unite all of South Africa under one Dutch government and when he eventually failed to achieve this dream (as President of the Transvaal from 1883 to 1900), he spent the last years of his life in exile.

Cecil Rhodes went to South Africa originally in hope that the climate would be beneficial to the malady of tuberculosis which had afflicted him since childhood. It was, and after a year and at the age of eighteen, he joined the rush to the diamond diggings. Smarter and luckier than many others, Rhodes made a small fortune almost immediately and returned to England to improve his neglected education, earning a degree from Oxford. He thereafter returned to the diamond mines and built up his small wealth until he was in the millionaire class.

Like Kruger, he had a dream. Originally, it was that

Britain should rule the world; finally, he settled for a smaller goal—that Britain should rule the entire continent of Africa. He formed the British South Africa Company, which was eventually given a royal charter. He persuaded the British government to take over huge parts of Southern Africa, either by direct annexation or through his company. He organized the great De Beers Consolidated Mines Company with himself as Chairman. He was Prime Minister of Cape Colony from 1890 to 1896.

Oddly, in the days of the early English-Dutch struggle it was Rhodes and the British who won, yet today it is the descendants of the old Boers who rule South Africa.

The discovery of diamonds and then gold in South Africa completely transformed the country. Until the first diamond was found on the banks of the Vaal River, most of South Africa's people were subsistence farmers and cattle growers, both black and white, although admittedly the whites had the easier time. But even they lived close to their land, seldom leaving it, growing their own food, making their own clothes, and seldom traveling farther then an occasional visit to a neighbor.

The discovery of diamonds in the Cape Province about 1870 started the change. In just a few months it brought thousands of emigrants from England and other parts of Europe as well as from Africa itself. Within four years, Kimberley, which previously had been a barren land, was the second largest city in South Africa and by 1880 more than $100 million worth of diamonds had been taken from the ground by the crudest of crude methods used in the earliest mining days.

While the rural culture of South Africa was still reeling under the impact of the diamond seekers, gold was discovered on the Witwatersrand (Ridge of White Water) in the Transvaal. The appeal of searching for diamonds pales beside the lure of the magic cry of gold. Where the discovery of diamonds brought prospectors by the hundreds, the discovery of gold brought them by the thousands and then by the hundreds of thousands. It was not a phenomenon unique to South Africa. The United States saw the same mad scramble in California in 1849 and again in the Klondike and other parts of Alaska in the 1890s.

Within ten years after the first gold was found on the Witwatersrand River, the mining camp in the empty highlands south of Pretoria had become a mining city of 100,000 people with thousands more scattered about the perimeters. Today that camp is Johannesburg, the second largest city in all of Africa, second only to Cairo.

The two governments sharing control of South Africa took radically different views of the gold and diamond discoveries, and of the almost parallel appearance of cheap and easy-to-mine coal which appeared in 1887. The Dutch under Kruger saw the giant emigration of types so different from themselves as a threat—as it was —to their vastly independent and in many ways pleasantly placid way of life. The British saw it in terms of finance and industrialization; indeed, foreign capital was already beginning to pour in.

These factors alone might have led to war between the

English and the Dutch for control, but the deciding factor probably was completely new and unforeseen: Germany intervened by landing an exploring group on the Atlantic coast some six hundred miles above Capetown, claiming crown rights to the whole of South West Africa and proposing to build a railroad across to the eastern coast. Kruger was pro-German and put out the welcome mat. England was aghast.

Moved by thoughts of manifest destiny, the rights of empire, and the unceasing urgings of Cecil Rhodes, Britain began annexing lands right and left to block the Germans and also any expansion of the Boer provinces. The Boers in turn were making life miserable for these *uitlanders* who had virtually taken over the day-to-day life of their land. The result of all of these conflicting cultures and interests led inevitably to the Boer War which began in October, 1899.

In the early days of the struggle the Boers had the advantage of both numbers and leadership, and they were consistently victorious until an alarmed London government sent in reinforcements from England, India, and the Middle East under the leadership of Field Marshal Frederick Sleigh Roberts and later Lord Kitchener. The tide of war changed to a British triumph. A treaty of peace was concluded on May 31, 1902.

The cessation of hostilities was followed by the South African National Convention and the Act of Union, completed in 1910, which formed the Union of South Africa. The Union had four provinces: Cape Colony, Natal, just above it, the Transvaal, and the Orange Free

State. Each province had a certain amount of autonomy.

Ironically, the much more liberal English-speaking in Cape Colony and Natal believed quite sincerely that their spirit of liberalism would spread eventually over the two Boer states. Actually, it has been the other way around; the apartheid policies of the Boers now dominate the policies of the entire country.

By the latter half of the 1970 decade the whites in South Africa felt themselves a nation embattled, with the Damoclean sword of a civil war seemingly very real indeed. Such a war would pit the nation's four million first-class white citizens against 20 million second-class black and colored citizens. If the whites were not to be overcome by the sheer weight of numbers they would have to slaughter the blacks in such quantity that the civilized world would never tolerate them thereafter.

The alternative, of course, was change, and the government leaders showed no real willingness to do anything but toughen their police role as the unrest grew, and to reassert their policy of white supremacy. Since 1948, when the Afrikaner Nationalist Party came to power, the official rule was that South Africa has four races—white, black, Asian, and mixed (colored)—and they should be separate and unequal, politically, socially, and mostly geographically.

The stand of the Afrikaner—and it had to a surprising degree the tacit (if rarely admitted) concurrence of the English-speaking whites in South Africa—was that he had just as valid a claim to his country as any other group, black or white. The claim has logic. The white

Afrikaner settled the land on the Cape at least as early as the present-day blacks. He came early and stayed, occupying the land, much of which he had to clear of even earlier settlers, but that was not unusual in those days.

The Dutch-descended Afrikaners and the English-descended "English-speaking" (again, for lack of a better term) have clung to their ancestry to a remarkable extent, considering the fact that they have been occupying the same country to some degree or other for more than a century and several generations. The English-speaking still consider themselves English and think of England as the homeland. The Dutch, on the other hand, are Afrikaners, native to and part of South Africa, with no feelings of kinship toward the Netherlands. During World War II, when Holland was the victim of German aggression, there was no violent sympathetic reaction among the Afrikaners. Many of them, in fact, sided with the Axis powers. The Afrikaners of today actually constitute Africa's white tribe, which could, as the *London Economist* points out, become Africa's lost tribe.

The answer which destroys the Afrikaner's presumed logic of white supremacy is, of course, that in this nation of South Africa there are others with corresponding rights and that no group of humans should hope—or even want—to become the absolute masters of another group of humans. This basic tenet is only compounded by the fact that the whites are ruling, and far less than benignly, a body of humans which outnumbers them some six to one.

South Africa has two languages today, English and Afrikaans, which is the official language and which is used in all schools. The African language is used only in the homelands or tribal areas—Zulu, Sotho, and so on. The government has the traditional three branches: the Executive with a president elected for seven years, a two-section Legislative branch and a Prime Minister who is chief executive, and the Judiciary. South Africa has the highest literacy rate in the continent: whites, virtually 100 percent; nonwhites between 50 and 85 percent.

South Africa is a relatively poor crop-raising nation, due to the erratic rainfall, and has only a fair fishing industry, despite its long coastline, but makes up for those deficiencies in its vast mineral wealth. The country's monetary unit is the rand, worth $1.50 at the official exchange rate.

The gross national product in 1974 was 21,657 billion rand, of which minerals made up the considerable bulk. Figures for that year set gold sales at 2,559,810 billion rand, one and a half times that amount if you count it in dollars. Copper sales were 204,895 million rand; coal, 199,852 million; and diamonds, 142,662 million. Silver, iron, manganese, chrome, and asbestos ranged lower.

Gross national product in 1974 was about 700 rand per capita. That income, however, is very unevenly divided, with a considerable differential between white and nonwhite, or skilled and nonskilled. In manufacturing, the differential in 1975 was 4.7 to 1 in manufacturing and 9.3 to 1 in mining and quarrying.

Despite inflation, which has reached South Africa as

well as the Western world, this land which seems to be clinging tenaciously to another age, is still a minor paradise for the middle-class white with a middle-class income. It is one of the rapidly shrinking number of places in the world where he has been able to enjoy life in its grand old manner. It is quite easy to understand his reluctance to give it up, and to speculate that, perhaps, much of the world's antagonism is mixed with envy.

South Africa is a land where garden parties and afternoon teas are still a symbol of gracious living and where dinner parties are usually black tie. Inflation may have forced the average small apartment dweller to get along with one servant instead of two and the suburban executive to cut down from the former complement of five— cook, houseboy-driver, butler, maid, and gardener, with the latter also taking care of the swimming pool. But homes are graceful and well-maintained with meticulously cared-for gardens.

There are scores of private clubs with the normal amenities of tennis, golf, pool, dining facilities, and often libraries. There are riding clubs and fox hunting. Rugby and soccer have a large spot in the sporting life. The theater is popular, as is opera, both encouraged by South Africa's society as a whole, along with painting, dancing, sculpture, and other arts.

South Africa is also a storybook land of some of the grandest scenery in the world: scores of lakes and hundreds of miles of beaches, some famous for surfing; the glorious grandeur of the Drakensberg Range and, of course, the national parks, including the Kruger which has more than a thousand lions along with giraffes, waterbucks, and the monumental rhinoceros, reputedly a shy, timorous animal though few people care about testing that theory.

On the other hand, today—or up through 1977 at least —the entire lives of black Africans are regulated socially, economically, and politically. They are prohibited from working at a large number of skilled jobs in mining and industry. The white government tells them where, when, and at what they may work. The government sets the wage, normally far less than a black worker could earn were he white. The nonwhite African has no union, no bargaining power, and no right to strike. In certain instances it is a criminal offense for him to be absent from his job.

The nonwhite—and this includes the colored and the Indians—is forbidden to marry a white. The black and colored cannot own land except, sometimes, in a designated ghetto to which he is assigned (or in his new homeland when it becomes operative). He cannot move about the country without official permission. He has a passbook which he must carry at all times and produce to any policeman on demand. Not having the passbook normally results in arrest and a fine. Most hotels and restaurants are segregated. There are separate doors for white and black in many public buildings, separate sections in parks and on beaches.

To meet, after a fashion, the rising demands of the nonwhites for a fair share of the country's basic wealth and for an equal voice in its political power, the South

African government has divided the country into segments, allotting themselves (with less than 17 percent of the population) just over 81 percent of the territory, including all of the cities, the ports, the industrial centers, and mines. The blacks, with 71 percent of the population, receive just under 13 percent of the territory, while the colored and Asians, with just over 12 percent of the people, live in segregated areas, mostly on the outskirts of the cities.

To avoid the confusion of Afrikaner and African and the similarity of their spelling, the white people of South Africa have lumped all black Africans there under the ethnic term of Bantu, an enormous black tribal unit to which all of them do not belong. In the division of the South African territory, the government has created nine *bantustans,* each of which is intended to be the homeland of a tribe or language group.

None of the *bantustans,* or homelands, are single entities, but range in segments of land from two (Transkei) to twenty-nine (KwaZulu). The population density averages 121 persons per square mile, though the average in South Africa as a whole, and for all people, is only 34. More than half the male labor force in the *bantustans* will be working in white areas. Most of these men also will reside in white areas by choice or economic necessity. Many other tribal members simply do not want to live in their prescribed homelands. In many instances they live in the cities and have never been near their assigned *bantustan.* However, though they may spend their lives living out of the assigned tribal homeland, they will be

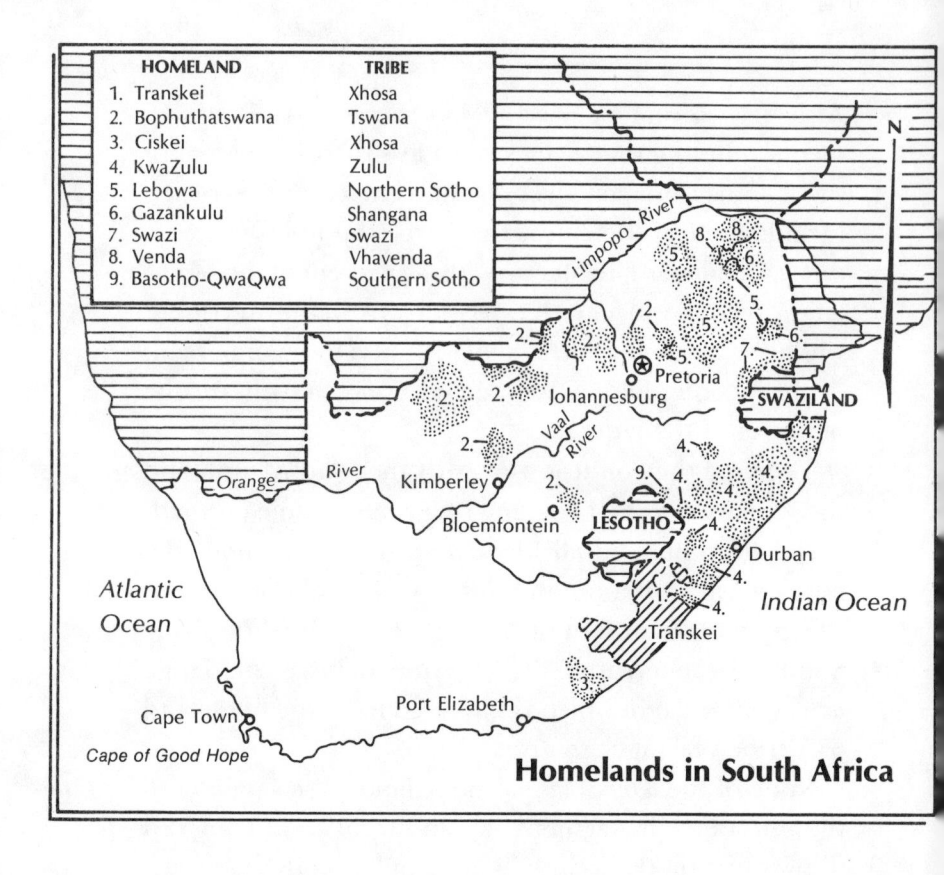

HOMELAND	TRIBE
1. Transkei	Xhosa
2. Bophuthatswana	Tswana
3. Ciskei	Xhosa
4. KwaZulu	Zulu
5. Lebowa	Northern Sotho
6. Gazankulu	Shangana
7. Swazi	Swazi
8. Venda	Vhavenda
9. Basotho-QwaQwa	Southern Sotho

Homelands in South Africa

citizens there and cannot hope ever to become citizens of the nation of South Africa.

Only two of the *bantustans* had been opened by late 1977. Transkei, now the "independent" home of the Xhosa tribe, was the first. On a rainy Monday in late October of 1976, in a ceremony as somber as the mood of the participating black officials, the flag of South Africa was lowered and the banner of Transkei raised. Then, in December of 1977, the homeland of Bophuthatswana became the second in line, this time in a ceremony held at midnight and to the accompaniment of a 101-gun salute and tribal dances.

Transkei, with only one short break in its territorial integrity, comes close to being a single entity and has a coastline stretching along the Indian Ocean. Bophuthat-swana, on the other hand, consists of seven landlocked pieces of territory scattered over two South African states and 500 miles. It is the homeland of the Tswana tribe.

Thus far the two *bantustans* have been recognized diplomatically by one nation—South Africa—and by each other. When the ninth homeland becomes independent it will mean that no black will be a citizen of South Africa —if indeed any are today.

The *bantustans* and their tribal people are:

HOMELAND	TRIBE
Transkei	Xhosa
Bophuthatswana	Tswana
Ciskei	Xhosa
KwaZulu	Zulu
Lebowa	Northern Sotho
Gazankulu	Shangaan-Tsonga
Swazi	Swazi
Venda	Vhavenda
Basotho-QwaQwa	Southern Sotho

Southwest of Johannesburg is the suburban ghetto of Soweto. Before World War II it was a small black community, a slum but manageable. During the war the city's booming industrial development brought a demand for more and more manpower and the blacks flowed into Johannesburg by the tens of thousands, expanding Soweto tremendously and creating an enormous housing problem.

At first Soweto was a collection of squatter shacks, the same kind one sees on the perimeters of Latin American cities, the *barrios* of the country peasants who have fled unproductive land to seek something they hope will be better in the cities.

Soweto is now a community of a million, perhaps more, totally black. Forced by the threat of epidemics, the governments of South Africa and Johannesburg combined to build sewer lines, disposal plants, and roads. More than 10,000 homes were built (some temporary) and schools. Some of the homes have electricity, most do not. They are crowded, dreary, and most have only outdoor plumbing.

Soweto has become, in South Africa, the center and the symbol of black revolt. The seed and the spirit of rebellion in South Africa's blacks had lain dormant for a decade—two decades, perhaps—until the latter half of the 1970s when the rioting began. It started with the schoolchildren (52 percent of Soweto's population is under the age of twenty-five) and in the first serious revolt, in June of 1976, almost half of the blacks arrested, killed (four that day, almost 400 since), or injured badly enough to be sent to hospitals were below the age of sixteen and most of the rest not over twenty-four.

The rioting has spread to other parts of the nation,

despite the efforts of the South African security forces, who arrested the student leaders by the hundreds and forced hundreds more to flee the country.

On June 23, 1977, tens of thousands of students demonstrated in Soweto while other hundreds slipped into Johannesburg by bus (instead of marching) and demonstrated by marching on police headquarters, all protesting the double standard in black and white education. One student was killed by police in Soweto, several injured, and 130 arrested in Johannesburg. They carried signs, one addressed to Daniel Sechaba Monsitsi, former president of the Soweto Students' Representative Council and held in "detention" by the police. The sign read: "Sechaba, a child by the name of Uhuru [freedom] is about to be born by Mother Azania [South Africa]. Don't commit suicide. You have a taste of freedom in store."

Almost two dozen blacks have died in "police detention" and until the Stephen Biko case the police called it suicide. Biko was a young moderate political activist who preached that his fellow African blacks must first learn to respect themselves through education, activities, and achievements before they could expect the respect of the rest of the world.

Biko was arrested in the late summer of 1977 and then on September 12 the South African Security Police announced that he had died of head injuries in a struggle with police. The resulting outcry from both inside and outside South Africa resulted in an investigation and inquest finally being ordered. It was carried out by Magistrate Marthinus J. Prins over a three-week period at the end of which, on December 2, Prins announced his findings.

The evidence, Prins said, had proved that Biko had indeed died in a struggle with police. He added that "available evidence does not prove the death was brought about by any act or omission involving an offense by any person."

Testimony at the inquest had described how Biko had been kept in iron shackles, made to lie on a urine-soaked mat and driven 700 miles in a jolting Land-Rover vehicle while in a semiconscious state. Coincidentally, only hours before the verdict was announced, Biko's brother and cousin were arrested in a raid on the home of an Anglican priest in Soweto, the Johannesburg black ghetto.

The United States strongly denounced the verdict, saying that the black leader had been "a victim of flagrant neglect and official responsibility." The State Department said it was "shocked."

It has been pointed out that the black man in South Africa is probably better off than in any other spot on the continent. He lives in the economically richest nation in Africa. He can almost always find work. He is the best educated (even with the double standard) and the best fed. His ghetto home may be better than he would find in another African country.

But, he is also the world's most clearly defined second-class citizen. He lacks any semblance of the thing that is now denied him by a policy of brutal suppression: the right to live with dignity, the right to live in freedom.

CHAPTER 6

Namibia

NAMIBIA LIES on the western coast of Southern Africa, embraced by two great deserts which bracket the troubled nation like two giant reversed parentheses. The Namib Desert on the west, from whence the country gets its name, is a true desert with the largest sand dunes in the world. It looks like the setting of every Foreign Legion picture ever made. The Kalahari Desert on the east is more rolling scrub and grazable grassland. It was the home of the Bushmen, the first documented citizens to have peopled the area. They still live there.

Namibia was formerly South West Africa and as such has been under the heavy thumb of neighboring South Africa since the victors got around to dividing up the world after World War I.

It is a rather spacious country with an area of more than 300,000 square miles, about the size of Texas and Louisiana if you combined the two states. The capital is Windhoek with a population of just over 60,000. Other

towns are Keetmanshoop, Tsumeb, Otjiwarongo, Swa-
kopmund, and Lüderitz. The population is close to 800,
000 with black Africans having 88 percent of that number, whites just over 11 percent, and coloreds less than
1 percent.

Germany shocked the smugly well-entrenched South
African Dutch and English whites in 1883 by landing at
Lüderitz on the Atlantic coast just above Cape Town. A
year later they announced they were annexing the whole
of South West Africa. England had already blocked off a
434-square-mile enclave around the only good harbor
on the west coast at Walvis Bay, and the German move
led to ticklish negotiations between the governments of
Bismarck and Victoria. Germany's "Iron Chancellor"
backed away from Walvis Bay claims and the British
crown agreed to recognize the rest of South West Africa,
from the Atlantic to the 20th-degree longitude, as a
"German Sphere of Influence." However, when Germany announced her intention of building a rail line to
the Indian Ocean, across what Cecil Rhodes called "the
Suez Canal route of Southern Africa," Britain promptly
annexed or took over as a protectorate the territory bordering the new German colony on the east—Bechuanaland, now Botswana. This, of course, was the country
across which Germany had planned to build the railroad
and abruptly ended that idea.

As had happened in South Africa, the German whites
after a few years began pushing their way inland in
search of new land and this led them inevitably into
conflict with the two major black tribes of the area—the

Herero and the Nama. The wars lasted from 1904 until 1907.

It was during the campaign against the Herero tribe that the troops of German General von Trotha carried out his infamous "extermination order" which resulted in the brutal slaughter of some 65,000 Herero tribal members. Having reduced this formerly prosperous cattle-raising people to a 15,000 remnant, the German settlers in true colonial fashion took over their land and animals and impressed the Herero tribesmen as laborers on their own seized lands.

The League of Nations came into being after the first World War and in 1920 formally decreed that South West Africa should not be tossed up for grabs as a spoils of war but should be a "sacred trust of civilization." Then the League devised an innovative governing device which became immediately popular with the winning side until well after the next World War. The device was "mandate" and was widely employed around the world, particularly in Africa and the Middle East.

So South West Africa became a mandate of South Africa. The act unintentionally gave South Africa a means of installing an apartheid control over the mandated blacks, which reduced them to a less then benign form of serfdom. Segregation, white over black, as well as discrimination, was total. Whether the mandate actually gave the South African whites the power to do this legally didn't really much bother the people governing. They just continued doing what the Germans had been doing, only more competently. In 1933 the South African government petitioned the League for the right to annex their mandate, but the League refused. The Mandates Commission, as a matter of fact, for some years had disapproved the administrative measures carried out by the South Africans but had no powers to do more than disapprove.

The League of Nations, of course, ceased to be after World War II. It was superceded by the United Nations and the mandate system was superceded by the trustee system.

South Africa's first move, when the United Nations became active in the early 1950s, was to petition again to be allowed to annex South West Africa. This was declined but when the UN then requested that South West Africa be placed under a UN trusteeship, South Africa reversed itself and balked on the grounds that the UN was not the automatic successor of the old League of Nations and its authority was yet to be tested.

There has followed then for some twenty-five years a series of decisions, nondecisions, and reversals by the United Nations and the International Court of Justice which, as sociologist-author Ruth First, writing for Europa Publications, said "was to prove demonstrably the hiatus between moral assertion and effective action by the world body."

These various maneuvers included at least five resolutions in the United Nations condemning South Africa's actions in Namibia, an International Court decision that South Africa's presence in Namibia was illegal, the dispatching of two UN representatives to Namibia to convey

the UN point of view, and the naming of two commis-
sioners with authority to take over the administration of
Namibia's government.

During most of this quarter of a century the government of South Africa never actually took a stance of
defying the United Nations; South Africa simply didn't
comply with any of the UN plans nor appear to hear any
of the resolutions of condemnation.

On the contrary, during the years of 1968 and 1969,
South Africa completed the incorporation of Namibia
into the parent country. This included taking control of
Namibia's foreign affairs and national defense; all administration down to the local level, including police; all
transport, immigration, customs, and the chores con-
nected with the collection and retention of tax monies.
This was given the color of legality by the South West
Affairs Act of 1969 passed by the government of Prime
Minister Vorster in Cape Town, which made Namibia the
fifth province of South Africa. It also covered, naturally,
control of all revenues, commerce, industry, labor, mining, and health, and extended to Namibia South Africa's
own security laws. These included the authority to detain
"political suspects" for an indefinite length of time without the right of habeas corpus.

During the four or five years ending in 1972, a special
commission named by the South African government
and given the task of dealing with the apartheid problem
in Namibia had come up with a plan similar to that
adopted in South Africa, of dividing the country up into
homelands, or *bantustans*. The plan specified eight home-

lands comprising 29.65 percent of the land for blacks. Of the remaining land, 44.1 percent would be for whites and the remainder would be state lands. A wave of strikes and rioting followed announcement of the *bantustans,* and then the first attempts to implement the homelands plan. The unrest continued and in the spring of 1974, South Africa conscripted Namibian blacks to police borders and to bring tribal authorities into efforts to stop the protests and disquiet. The result was a wave of brutality, blacks against blacks. Some 15,000 Africans, mostly students and teachers from the border province of Kvambo, fled into Zambia.

In September of 1975 the South African government convened a government conference in the Turnhalle building in Windhoek (which became known in time as the Turnhalle Conference), composed of both black and white delegates, to come up with a formula for governing the country. The white delegates were named by the South African government. The blacks, some named, some tribal leaders, some elected, were all moderates and known to be comfortable working within the framework of the present system.

In March of 1977, South African Prime Minister Vorster announced the results of the conference, i.e., that a new Namibian government could be worked out based on a three-tier or three-level system. Control at the top would, of course, always remain in the hands of the whites.

A month after this announcement from Turnhalle, the five Western members of the National Security Council of the United Nations—Canada, France, the United Kingdom, the United States, and West Germany—for the first time sat down together and decided to act in concert on the problem of South Africa. The five, who became known as the Contact Group, in addition to being the Western nations to which South Africa had the strongest cultural ties, were also—and perhaps more importantly—South Africa's biggest trading partners.

Acting, they said, as five nations who happened also to be members of the UN Security Council, they informed South Africa that they each found the Turnhalle results totally unacceptable.

Soon thereafter the Western powers presented their own independence plan for the captive country. It called for an immediate cease-fire, a phased withdrawal of all South African troops (to be replaced by United Nations forces), an immediate halt to discriminatory law enforcement, and for elections leading to Namibian independence by the end of 1978.

Possibly shocked by this show of unified moral and economic strength, South Africa agreed.

The plan, however, ran into immediate opposition from the South West Africa People's Organization (SWAPO), a formidable Marxist-oriented and Angola-based guerrilla group. SWAPO President Sam Nujoma laid down certain points which he said must be met for SWAPO to agree to (and not sabotage) the Western plan. They centered around the release of political prisoners and the withdrawal of South African armed forces.

SWAPO and Vorster's government each questioned

the other's sincerity. When South Africa in May of 1978 staged a bloody raid on a SWAPO camp deep in Angola, Nujoma called it an attempt to thwart any agreement. South Africa in turn accused Nujoma of wanting to set up a Marxist military dictatorship. Then in July SWAPO accepted the Western plan, a start toward agreement.

Namibia is a healthy place, with a hot, dry climate, too hot for profitable farming except in the northern provinces, though this could be corrected with more modern technology.

The gross national product of Namibia is just under $1 billion. It has an eminently respectable diamond production, is one of the top ten uranium-producing countries in the world, and has other mineral resources of copper, lead, and zinc. It is also one of the world's largest karakul (or caracul) sheep-raising nations. The hides of the karakul sheep appear in the Western markets in the form of Persian lamb coats and jackets, both popular items of female attire.

South Africa has mingled the trade figures of Namibia with her own for several years, so it is not possible to know exactly what they are, but they should be respectable. And Namibia has been a harnessed market for South Africa since the beginning of the original mandate after World War I, selling her people canned foodstuffs and hardware and mechanical items, from small tools to industrial machinery.

CHAPTER 7

Rhodesia

A THOUSAND YEARS or so ago, long before the great wave of European exploration, the Moslems of the Persian Gulf were sending great sharp-prowed dhows with their single billowing lateen sail into the Indian Ocean in quest of trade with India and with Africa's eastern coast.

In the course of this they established settlements along the African coastline to serve both as rest and supply stops and trading ports. By the thirteenth century there were half a dozen of these, now grown into city states and some of them extraordinarily rich and powerful. Attracted by this prosperity, the enterprising Bantu blacks, who were engaged in their great migration from the north, moved into the cities and commingled with the Moslem Arabs to create their own culture and the language of the East Coast—Swahili. Ranging downward along the coast were the city kingdoms of Malindi and Mombasa and, of course, Zanzibar, now part of Tanzania and one of the world's leading producers of cloves. Even farther on down was the island kingdom of Kilwa, a great medieval city which drew its wealth from ivory and the trade with India, but more—and in enormous quantity— from the gold which was brought in from Zimbabwe, now Rhodesia.

Landlocked Rhodesia is bounded on the north by the Zambesi River and on the south by the Limpopo. The land between, which the black Africans have always known as Zimbabwe, is a highland plateau on three levels. The Bantu tribes used it in their great migrations southward long before the white man arrived, probably about A.D. 1000.

The Bantu found the land already occupied by Bushmen and Hottentots, who had probably reached the same area some five hundred years earlier. And they, in turn, may have replaced still other tribes, for man—or his upright ancestor—is believed to have lived in Central and Southern Africa for as long as two million years.

The tribes the Bantu found had progressed from being simply nomadic hunter-gatherers to living at least a portion of the year in small villages where they kept cattle and practiced a primitive form of crop raising. Recent excavations have revealed that the village huts were made of mud and were built around a central enclosure with the entirety surrounded by a dense thorn tree wall to keep out marauders, both two- and four-legged.

The first Bantu people to arrive were probably members of the Shona (also called Mashona) tribe. They too were farmers and herders but had emerged many years back from the Stone Age to the Age of Iron. They took the pottery skills of the Bushmen and the Hottentots and improved on them; they opened up mines—copper, iron, and gold—and added metal tools and weapons, along with ornaments. They instituted a more rigid form of government, began the construction of solid walled communities, and started trading, first with neighbors and then the outside world.

By far the greatest of the communities built by the Shona tribes, probably in the twelfth to the fourteenth centuries, was the granite-structured city of Zimbabwe from which the country later took its name and which may have been the capital of a great kingdom. The kingdom was known, legendarily, as Monomatapa and remained as the center of the cult of the god Mwari, as late as the early 1800s. Ruins of the walled city are located near present-day Fort Victoria.

Shona history, all orally transmitted, maintains that Mwari, widely worshipped as a rainmaker, had a number of mortal descendants who ruled Zimbabwe, including a great-great grandson named Nyatsimba, whose military campaigns were so successful he earned the title of "Ravager of the Lands." Nyatsimba built up a great empire which was bordered by the Zambesi and the Limpopo rivers but which stretched thousands of miles from the Kalahari Desert (in present lower Botswana) to the Indian Ocean.

The word "Zimbabwe" in the Shona language means "great place" or "houses of stone," either of which, or both, fittingly describe the city as it was. Its ruins today identify it as a walled fortress, large enough to have maintained several thousand people. Its principal structure was a great temple with elliptical walls thirty feet tall, its stones fitted without mortar.

Zimbabwe's greatest power and glory probably came in the sixteenth century when it was the ruling place of the Rosvis, a dynasty of kings who established the trade of gold with Kilwa which brought an endless flood of wealth to the country. The glory of Zimbabwe ended in the early nineteenth century in successive raids from the fierce Zulu tribes farther south.

The Rhodesia of today lies inland in south-central Africa, bordered on the north and east by Zambia and Mozambique, on the west by Botswana, and on the south by South Africa.

Physically, Rhodesia is largely high plateau country with three distinct gradations. The "high veld" crosses the country, southwest-northeast at four to five thousand-feet altitude. The "middle veld" flanks the high veld at three to four thousand feet. And the "low veld" occupies the Limpopo and Sabi-Lundi basin in the south and southeast, plus the Zambezi in the north. A steep mountainous escarpment rises in the east to form the border with Mozambique.

Rhodesia has an area of 150,333 square miles, which makes the country about the size of England or the state of Montana. It lies within the tropics but its altitude makes the climate subtropical. In winter months—that is, May until August—the temperature range is from 37 to 47 degrees Fahrenheit and in summer—September

1. John Vorster, Prime Minister of South Africa

2. *After his inauguration in 1975 as South Africa's third State President, Dr. N. Diederichs met with leaders of the country's homelands.*

3. *View of Cape Town with Houses of Parliament in the foreground*

4. *A Zulu chieftain*

5. *View of Johannesburg. At bottom left is the old Johannesburg Fort built by Paul Kruger.*

6. Buying fruit at the Indian market in Durban, South Africa

7. Timber is a thriving industry in South Africa.

8. A fishing boat unloads its catch at Walvis Bay in Namibia (South West Africa).

9. Ian Smith, Prime Minister of Rhodesia

10. *Shangaan men doing a tribal dance in Rhodesia*

11. *An aerial view of Zimbabwe, the ancient capital of Rhodesia. The ruins lie within Zimbabwe National Park.*

12. *Victoria Falls, one of the world's greatest tourist attractions, is 350 feet high and over a mile wide.*

13. *The Western world depends on Southern Africa for vitally important minerals. This is a chrome mine in Rhodesia.*

14. *Kenneth Kaunda, President of Zambia*

15. Tobacco is one of the chief exports of Malawi.

16. A nitrogen factory in Zambia

17. His Majesty Sobhuza II, King of Swaziland

18. *Maphevu Dlamini, Prime Minister of Swaziland*

19. *Tourism is encouraged in Southern African countries. Above, road signs in Swaziland.*

20. H. Kamuzu Banda, Life President of Malawi

21. Ceremonies at Kamuzu Stadium in Blantyre as Dr. Banda was sworn in as Life President in 1966

22. Government office buildings at Lilongwe, capital of Malawi

23. *Since independence, pride in the nation's cultural heritage has been revived in Malawi.*

24. *Tourists relax at a resort at Lake Malawi.*

through March—from 80 to 100 degrees. Rains come in the summer, an average of 25 to 30 inches a year.

The population of Rhodesia, largely by estimation, consists of about 5,800,000 Africans, 275,000 whites of European origin (mostly English), and 29,300 Asians and colored or mixed. The African blacks are divided into two Bantu linguistic groups, the Matabele and Mashona. There are also minor tribal units: Sena, Venda, Sotho, Tonga, and Hlengwe.

Though the early Portuguese were the first white men to reach Southern Africa, they rarely ventured inland and thus it was not until the nineteenth century that a few explorers and more missionaries made their way into Zimbabwe, found the ruins of the great walled fortress, and confirmed what earlier explorers had already claimed—that the country abounded in gold mines which were already, many of them, working.

By the latter part of the century the area had been pretty well occupied by Cecil Rhodes' British South Africa Company which, in 1890, was granted a royal charter by an English government very reluctant to assume direct control of the area for a number of reasons, chiefly the expense and the difficulty of any kind of policing responsibility. The British did, however, take the precaution of limiting Rhodes' managers by giving the white settlers a strong voice on a newly established Legislative Council. This representation grew into a majority when Rhodes, realizing that the gold output was not as great as he had hoped, began to encourage white farming as a second source of revenue. By 1907 the farmers had a majority on the Council and in 1914 took over the company's powers. In acquiescing to this move, the British expected Rhodesia to become a part of the country of South Africa, but in 1922 a majority of the white settlers voted to become instead a self-governing colony. Under a constitution written the following year, the British retained certain rights, most important being the right of veto over constitution and discrimination matters.

By 1978, Rhodesia had several names, but legally was Southern Rhodesia, a self-governing colony of Great Britain whose current government was in revolt against the British Crown. The events leading up to this position began with the Land Apportionment Act in 1930, which made the first division of the country—and not quite equally—into two racially exclusive parts. The black Africans in their allotted area were prohibited from competing in the market with their produce and instead were forced to sell it to white buyers at preset prices. They were barred from the unions which gave the white workers great bargaining powers, reducing the role of black workers to the status of powerless, migrant laborers.

Then, in 1953 after a referendum, Southern Rhodesia joined Northern Rhodesia and Nyasaland to form the Federation of Rhodesia and Nyasaland. In 1963, ten years later, this federation was dissolved by the British government which, the following year, granted Northern Rhodesia and Nyasaland independence. They became, respectively, the Republics of Malawi and Zambia, fully independent black African nations.

Conscious of its record of successful self-government for forty years, Southern Rhodesia also petitioned for independence. England, equally conscious of Rhodesia's record of white supremacy and black discrimination, and of the fact that the ruling whites represented less than 5 percent of the total population, declined.

So, on November 11, 1965, Rhodesia, having made what it considered to be the necessary amendments to its constitution, though omitting British concurrence, declared itself to be independent.

Following this unilateral declaration of independence, the British government declared the Rhodesian government to be without validity but also said it would not use force to end the rebellion. At the same time the United Nations also deemed the Rhodesian government illegal and called on member states to refrain from recognizing or assisting it. Then, a year later, the UN Security Council, for the first time in its history, imposed mandatory economic sanctions. Rhodesia's primary exports, including chrome, coal, gold, and tobacco, were placed on the forbidden list, along with shipments to Rhodesia of armaments, aircraft, and petroleum products. Two years later the sanctions were broadened into a virtual embargo (except for medical and educational materials).

Several conferences between British and Rhodesian government leaders brought no result and in 1969 the government of Prime Minister Ian Smith voted itself constitutional powers to again divide Rhodesia's land area between blacks and whites and to break the last formal ties with England by declaring the nation a republic.

The government then redivided Rhodesia under a new Land Tenure Act which became effective in 1970.

The land area of the country was split "equally," with 45 million acres going to 275,000 European whites and 45 million acres going to 5,900,000 African blacks. The European area contained the major cities, the transportation system, the industrial and mineral resource parts of the country, and the better farmlands.

Salisbury is the capital and largest city in Rhodesia and is the residence of almost half of the non-Africans in the countryside. The second city of Bulawayo claims most of the rest. Less than 15 percent of the non-African population lives in the country and the very extensive white land holdings are in charge of about 6,000 farmers or agribusinesses. Almost a million black Africans are employed in either urban mining and manufacturing or as household servants and farm laborers. Their individual annual earnings in 1978 were about a tenth that of the predominantly affluent middle-class whites.

Due to this availability of cheap black labor, accompanied by excellent business management, Rhodesia—like South Africa—has been for the past half century one of the more pleasant places for the middle-class white with a middle-class income to live a country club life from a multi-servanted home.

The new constitution of Rhodesia designated the President (replacing the Queen of England) as Chief of State. He was selected by the Executive Council or Cabinet. The Parliament consisted of a Senate and a House of Assembly. The House had fifty non-Africans elected by non-African voters, eight Africans elected by African voters, and eight Africans elected by tribal electoral colleges. The Senate had ten Europeans elected by the House, ten African chiefs elected by the Council of Chiefs, and three of any race appointed by the President. The Senate, patterned after the British House of Lords, had only delaying powers.

An earlier constitution provided for eventual majority rule. The newer constitution specifically prohibited the African majority from ever acquiring a dominate role in government and established separate voter lists—one for Europeans and one for Africans.

The executive branch of the Rhodesian government was virtually totally white as late as 1978—through a white Prime Minister and all of his fourteen supporting ministers. The government did give a brief curtsy toward black representation with a last place branch—the African Chiefs with Regional Responsibilities. There were places for four chiefs, not all of them always filled.

The President at that time was John James Wrathal. The Prime Minister and the man who ran Rhodesia, and had, since the elections of 1962 put his right-wing party in power, was Ian Smith.

The economy of Rhodesia has been rather under siege in the past few years, with sanctions taking a heavy toll and more and more of the country's income going for military expenses due to increasing guerrilla activities. Mozambique in 1976 recognized the sanctions imposition and closed its border, thus prohibiting Rhodesia from shipping via the Mozambique rail lines to the ports of Beira and Maputo (formerly Lourenço Marques). Since South Africa had already agreed to handle all Rhodesian shipping, this was not as important as was the loss of Mozambique as a customer.

The future fortunes in the economic field were uncertain, dependent on finding some solution to political problems via negotiations with the African National Council and upon how effective the sanctions can be. Rhodesia has a fine internal transportation system, good paved roads, and an effective electrical system. She has two-thirds of the world's known reserves of metallurgical-grade chromite. She also has large deposits of gold, coal, asbestos, copper, nickel, and iron. She has made a successful transition from being a purely mining and agricultural nation by adding industry during World War II.

Trade figures for Rhodesia have not been available since the employment of sanctions, and the last figure for gross national product was in 1974 when it was listed as 3,025 billion. Figures on employment and average earnings through that year were healthier than in most other nations of the world. And Rhodesia has been able to maintain its standard of living, according to all reports, by employing a system of trade known as the NCI, or "no currency involved." These are barter deals and exempt from controls.

In addition to the economic siege, Rhodesia has been, since 1972–73, under virtual military siege as well. Guerrilla forces in increasing numbers have been operating inside Rhodesia and, the Rhodesian authorities claimed,

from bases in both Mozambique and Zambia, using ter-
rorist tactics in random murders, often accompanied by
torture. In turn, Rhodesia has angered the governments
of both bordering countries by carrying out "hot pursuit" raids across their borders to attack, sometimes with
air support, camps and villages. The action so infuriated
the government of Zambia that it declared a state of war.
Mozambique, where most of the incidents have occurred, has declared the attack spots to be refugee
camps, and not guerrilla military supply bases.

In making a case for itself and its white vs. black policies, Rhodesians pointed out that their Land Tenure Act
which gave the nation's blacks half the land area of the
country was vastly better than the red Indians were ac-
corded in the United States; that the black literacy rate
of some 30 percent in its segregated schools was far
greater than in most of Africa; that the national income
of black workers in industry and business averages over
$700 a year (farm workers and servants earn about half
that); and adds that the record of other African governments following independence and the assumption of
black rule "has been a sorry one—civil war, tribalism,
blatant corruption, racism, starvation, and curtailment of
freedom."

In the late summer of 1976, under some pressure from
the government of South Africa, Prime Minister Ian
Smith agreed to a proposal made by then United States
Secretary of State Henry Kissinger for a biracial government in Rhodesia—which would mean black rule—
within two years.

The Kissinger proposal threw the matter back into the hands of Great Britain and resulted in the plan presented by Britain's Foreign Secretary, David Owen, in September, 1977, as recounted in Chapter 1.

One of the problems of the Owen Plan was that it asked all factions concerned to surrender too much power and control, this not only from the whites but from the black leaders who themselves were intransigently divided.

Of the five black political groups, the hard-line radicals were led by Joshua Nkomo and Robert Mugabe. Nkomo's African People's Union and Mugabe's African National Union together formed the Patriotic Front. Nkomo's rebels were based in Zambia, Mugabe's in Mozambique. Together their forces were numbered in the thousands and certainly Mugabe's, and probably Nkomo's, were trained by Cubans and armed by Russians.

The more moderate leaders were:

Bishop Abel Muzorewa, founder of the African National Council. Muzorewa probably had the largest popular following of all among Rhodesian blacks, who regarded him as above self-interest.

Ndabaningi Sithole, a self-proclaimed socialist, former ally but later a bitter enemy of Nkomo. Sithole attended theological college in the United States and was ordained there in 1955. His following was among students and intellectuals.

Jeremiah Chirau, a tribal chieftain, black member of the Rhodesian Senate, and leader of the Zimbabwe

United People's Organization. Chirau was one of four black senators denied visas to the United States for a speaking tour after the presentation of the Owen Plan, which America supported.

The Owen Plan had one effective result: it convinced Premier Ian Smith that the white rule of Rhodesia could not endure in its present form and to try, at least, for an acceptable alternative. As a result, he went into a long series of conferences with the moderate leaders, Muzorewa, Sithole, and Chirau, and on March 3, 1978, they announced that they had "reached agreement on certain fundamental principles to be embodied in a new constitution."

It was a detailed proposal which provided for majority rule on the basis of universal adult suffrage. Its critical points were listed as follows:

There will be a legislative assembly consisting of 100 members and the following provisions shall apply thereto:

(a) There will be a common voters' roll, with all citizens of eighteen and over being eligible for registration as voters, subject to certain recognized disqualifications.

(b) Seventy-two of the seats in the legislative Assembly will be reserved for blacks who will be elected by voters who are enrolled on the common roll.

(c) Twenty-eight of the seats in the legislative Assembly will be reserved for whites (i.e., Europeans as defined in the 1970 constitution) who will be elected as follows: Twenty will be elected on a preferential voting system by white voters who are enrolled on the common roll. Eight will be elected by voters who are enrolled on the common roll from sixteen candidates who will be nominated, in the case of the first Parliament, by an electoral college composed of the white members of the present House of Assembly and, in the case of any subsequent Parliament, by an electoral college composed of the twenty-eight whites who are members of the Parliament dissolved immediately prior to the general election.

An Executive Council was agreed upon to govern the nation and to release black political detainees, remove discrimination, draft a new constitution, create a climate for free and universal elections, and register voters. The Council was duly set up, composed of Smith and the three black conferees. The chairmanship was to rotate; Smith served first.

The results of Smith's move were mixed. Some detainees were released, many others remained in prison. Guerrilla leaders, unwilling to join the government but angered at being left out, stepped up the warfare. Thousands of whites liquidated belongings and left the country. Small arms target practice became a popular sport, but many whites here had always carried weapons.

Sometime in the fall of 1978, it was expected, the all-white voters' list would ballot on a new constitution based on the Smith plan. If they concurred, then the entire population over eighteen would vote. If both ballots carried and if no other eventuality occurred, the new independent nation of Zimbabwe was to be declared on December 31, 1978.

CHAPTER 8

Former Portuguese Africa

WHEN PRINCE HENRY the Navigator, son of King John I, died in 1460, he left his native Portugal a legacy of oceanic explorers unequalled in the world at that time. Henry, himself an advanced astronomer and mathematician, established an observatory and a school for geography and navigation. His star pupils explored the world, both east and west.

Among them were Diogo Cão, who landed at the mouth of the Congo (now Zaire) River and claimed modern Angola on the Atlantic for his king and country, and Vasco da Gama, who stopped off at Mozambique on the Indian Ocean on his way to finding a route to India via Southern Africa and did the same thing.

These two territories, both in today's Southern Africa, constitute two-thirds of what was until recently Portuguese Colonial Africa. (The third area was Portuguese Guinea, now the Republic of Guinea-Bissau, on the Atlantic coast of western Africa.)

Actually, even under the preemptive rights practiced by the great powers of the period, the Portuguese at best never had more than a faint "color of title" to the lands they claimed, and their colonial presence in Africa since the fifteenth century was a bit of national folkloric mythology. They put down a few settlements along the coastline and established what was known in that day as a "trading and raiding" practice along the edges of both oceans, particularly in Angola which they virtually depopulated in their greed for slaves.

Portugal's actual control over Mozambique and Angola did not begin until the late nineteenth century, affirmed by the Berlin Conference of 1884–85. This conference, attended by European nations, the United States, and Turkey, was called by Germany's Bismarck with the ostensible purpose of establishing free trade on the Congo and Niger rivers. Actually it was called more to settle the scramble for colonial rights on the so-called "dark continent." From this meeting Portugal emerged with a clear colonial title to her three countries, having been backed by the British, who didn't want any troubles over their own claims to retain Walvis Bay, South Africa, and the two Rhodesias. Belgium went along, too, for the conference recognized the incredible claims of the International Association, a private corporation of King Leopold II of Belgium, to most of the Congo.

The Portuguese do not have a sparkling record as colonists in Africa. Of course, none of the powers set exactly benign examples anywhere (including the colonizers of the United States), and Portugal was busy at the time getting a firm grip on Brazil. Even by the standards which existed well into the twentieth century, however, Portugal sat firmly at the bottom of the list of African developers.

She was the last to abolish slavery and even then substituted a system of enforced and unpaid labor which was about the same thing. She didn't build roads, establish schools or hospitals.

Portugal in her African colonial rule has always claimed great tolerance in accepting Africans as equals, always boasted of a policy of anti-racism. Unfortunately, both the tolerance and the policy were great in propaganda value but bore little reality to fact.

Census figures in 1950—which was just a year before Portugal made her African colonies states, promoting them from overseas territories—gave a truer picture of the Portuguese African population. The proportion which had become *asimilados* (achieved assimilated status), which, when recognized by the Portuguese, gave them the right to education above the lowest elementary level—and the right to exemption from enforced labor, thus treatment as human beings—was 0.75 in Angola, and just above 0.60 for Mozambique (only 0.03 in Guinea-Bissau).

It was this treatment, considerably worse even than the apartheid system of South Africa, which led to rebellion. The vast majority of the population of the Portuguese colonies (natives as distinguished from the few *asimilados*) were subject to impressed labor in their own countries or impressed "contract" labor in others. They had no right or chance of education. They could not organize. Even their occasional "cash crops" had to be sold on the Portuguese-controlled market at controlled prices. The revolt began in Angola in 1961 and in Mozambique in 1964. In the wake of the uprisings, Portugal attempted to establish reforms in the colonies, but they came too late.

By 1969 Portugal had almost her entire army engaged in the greatest of the African colonial wars—55,000 men in Angola and 60,000 in Mozambique.

Portugal's fighting forces were accompanied by some of the more sophisticated weapons of the era, weapons which had been supplied to the Portuguese under the NATO defense of Europe plan. The government of Portugal justified the use of these NATO weapons in Africa under the argument that both Angola and Mozambique had been made "states" of Portugal and were thus integral parts of the mother country.

Inevitably, of course, the colonies got outside help, and in 1975 Portugal was forced to grant independence to both Angola and Mozambique (as well as Guinea-Bissau).

The government of Portugal then found itself faced with another problem—the struggle to support nearly a million *retornados* who fled the African colonies, most of them settlers who were airlifted out at the last moment, leaving behind the farms and personal belongings they had accumulated over, in some cases, several generations. Already deeply in trouble with fiscal problems, including one of the highest rates of unemployment in Europe, the government in Lisbon had to meet this new problem of providing some $30 million a month to feed and house the refugee *retornados*.

CHAPTER 9

Angola

THE LAST QUARTER of a century has seen Angola, largest of the former Portuguese colonies, engaged in almost continuous armed fighting in what were actually two wars and repeated adventures into neighboring Zaire's troubles.

The first war was the prolonged struggle to overthrow the oppressive Portuguese rule. The date of its beginning can be set in 1958–59 and it continued until the Lisbon coup of 1974 when Portugal reversed its colonial policy and pulled its armed forces out of Africa.

The second war began in 1974 and was fought between the three major nationalist guerrilla factions which had been fighting for independence from Portugal—and sometimes against each other. This struggle came to an uneasy—and possibly not permanent—ending after a November 11, 1975, declaration of independence.

The first adventure into neighboring Zaire was in March, 1977, when an invading force from Angola swept into the adjacent province of Shaba, whose mineral

yields provide Zaire with 80 percent of her foreign earnings. There is considerable question as to how many of
the invaders were Angolans and how many were rebel-
lious Katangans. The province of Shaba was formerly
Katanga (hence, Katangans), and has been in a state of
smoldering and active rebellion for years. Many of the
rebels had taken refuge in Angola from their own government forces.

The second came in May, 1978, when a force of Katangans swept back into Shaba and quickly captured the
industrial town of Kolwezi, where some 2,000 Europeans
and perhaps a dozen Americans provided the technical
skills to operate the copper and cobalt industries there.

In the first incident, Zairean troops were able to pro-
tect the mining center from the rather ineffective raiders
until relief arrived—troops sent by King Hussein of Mo-
rocco.

The second invasion was well planned, led, and
trained. The rebel forces took Kolwezi in a matter of
hours and were preparing to move inland. Calling it a
rescue mission, several hundred Belgian troops and
French Foreign Legion paratroopers were flown in by
Belgium and France, with the United States providing
logistic aid.

The legionaires cleared the rebels from Kolwezi,
finding the bodies of a hundred or more Europeans
among others killed. The survivors were evacuated. The
mines had been flooded and would probably remain use-
less until Zaire's government could guarantee the safety
of the technicians and entice them back.

In each incident the troops were armed with Soviet

weapons. The second invasion brought a sharp rebuke from United States President Jimmy Carter. The President accused Cuba of training and arming the rebels and said that Cuba must share responsibility (with Russia) for the "bloody attacks."

By mid-1978 the Russian adventures in Africa had brought American-Soviet detente to its lowest point in years.

Angola is a complex nation with a turbulent history. It lies on the west coast of Southern Africa and has an area of 481,351 square miles, making it more than fourteen times the size of Portugal, the country which held it under colonial power for five centuries.

Geographically, Angola is divided into two parts: the nation proper, which lies south of the Zaire River, (formerly the Congo River), and the oil-wealthy enclave of Cabinda which is on the seacoast just north of Angola and separated from Angola proper by the Zaire River. Cabinda is covered by dense rain forest, while Angola proper is almost entirely a central plateau with an altitude of from three to four thousand feet which balances the tropical climate.

The white man discovered Angola in 1482, the discoverer being one of Portugal's master navigators, Diogo Cão, who arrived at the mouth of the Congo River to find the land under the rule of an African monarch who was, quite naturally, the King of the Congo (sometimes, then, Kongo). The Portuguese established friendly relations with the Congolese King on a second voyage in 1490 by sending a small fleet of ships carrying skilled workers, along with their tools, and priests.

The King accepted Christianity and sent his son, later the Congo's King Alfonso, to Lisbon to school. This rapport was of fairly short duration, however, for the Portuguese, finding no easily accessible gold or other treasure, began slaving rapaciously, taking the area's blacks to Brazil by the fleetload and forcing them to work in the colonies there. It has been estimated that as many as three million Angolan Africans were forcibly taken to Brazil and to other parts of South America by the Portuguese in more than three centuries of slave trading.

During these three hundred years the Portuguese rarely ventured far inland, depending on the native chieftains, bribed by trifles, to bring the slaves to the coast, particularly to the coastal town of Luanda, which the Portuguese had settled and which is now the capital of the country. The slaves were usually captives taken in the tribal wars—often little more than raids. The slaving was so prevalent during the seventeenth, eighteenth, and nineteenth centuries that it seriously depopulated the country. Even after World War I, when the Portuguese ventured from the coast to push their domination of the native blacks throughout the country, the inland control was always tenuous.

The convolutions of the various Angolan pursuits of independence and the civil struggles which followed ran a tortuous route. Weary as they were of the fighting, homesick and dispirited, Portugal's uniformed military in Angola probably had sufficient superiority in arms and training to have staved off the revolutionaries indefinitely had not a coup overthrown the regime of Portuguese dictatorship in 1974. The new government made a 180-degree turn in foreign policy and declared the African colonies were independent to form their own governments. And, a year later, it pulled out all of the Portuguese troops. Both the USSR and the United States gave aid to divergent factions during the civil war which followed the revolution. The American aid was negligible and it was undoubtedly the Soviet insertion of Cuban troops and massive arms shipments which turned the war's tide toward the victorious MPLA, the Popular Movement for the Liberation of Angola, led by Agostinho Neto.

Two other movements were formed, the Frente Nacional de Libertaccao de Angola (FNLA) and the Revolutionary Government in Exile (GRAE). Both received some support from the United States; both were eventually submerged by events.

Chief of these events was the action of Jonas Savimbi, who defected from GRAE (where he had held the title of "foreign minister") and formed the National Union for Total Independence of Angola (UNITA).

During the period of revolt against Portugal, UNITA and MPLA, and FNLA to a lesser degree, carried out three separate campaigns of guerrilla warfare, sometimes against the Portuguese military and occasionally against each other. The MPLA had its birth in Luanda in 1956. Its manifesto of purpose declared the organization's aims were to end a colonial system "which has implanted the microbes of ruin, hatred, backwardness, poverty, ignorance, and reaction" in Angola. A Soviet handbook, *Africa Today,* published in 1962, verifies that the MPLA was founded six years earlier on the "initiative of the Communist Party." Thus Soviet aims in Angola began quite early, working through Portugal's Communist party.

Testifying before the U.S. Senate much later, on February 6, 1976, William E. Schaufele, Jr., Assistant Secretary of State for African Affairs, explained the actions of both the Soviet Union and the United States in Angola.

"Based on my seventeen years of work with Africa," he said, "I am convinced that some consensus agreement could have been worked out bringing the factions together in Angola if they had been left to themselves. It was the Soviet decision, in my judgment, to step up arms aid to what it apparently regarded as an organization in which it had influence which destroyed . . . efforts to establish a provisional colonial government embracing the three factions."

Action of the United States to provide assistance to both the FNLA and UNITA forces, he said, was "reactive to those of the Soviet Union and Cuba, independent of the activities of South Africa (which involved itself later) and intended to promote a government of national unity."

The MPLA began receiving extensive Soviet military aid in late 1974 when it was still largely based just across the Zaire River in Brazzaville. The shipments of arms and other military equipment continued up until late 1975, according to the State Department. Up until early 1975 American aid to FNLA and UNITA (which eventually joined forces) was confined to money for political purposes. Said Assistant Secretary Schaufele: "The sum was doled out over many months and was insignificant compared to Moscow's military aid."

Then, when the Soviet arms began to arrive in a small flood, and when the MPLA reportedly refused all invitations to peace talks and ignored cease-fire invitations (and were being increasingly victorious in battle), the American decision not to supply arms aid was reversed and on July 18, 1975, "the use of covert funds for the FNLA and UNITA forces was authorized," Schaufele said. Whatever the CIA could have done at this stage was much too late to achieve the declared American aims, that is, to strengthen the FNLA-UNITA forces to preserve a military balance and bring about a compromise coalition government.

In August, 1975, and before American aid could be seriously effective, South Africa decided to take a hand, moving its forces through Namibia. The first move was to occupy dam sites which the South African government had held jointly with the Portuguese in Angola. Then, in September, for reasons of their own—quite possibly the spectre of a Communist nation next door—the South Africans shifted to military action against the MPLA.

It was at this time that large numbers of Cuban troops arrived in Angola, many of them as combat-trained and equipped units. And at about the same time (in action that probably was not coincidental) there was a marked increase in both the quantity and quality of Soviet and other Eastern European arms aid—rockets, mortars, tanks, and other armored vehicles—which poured in to be used by the Cubans. Their strength at that time was placed at from 10,000 to 20,000 men.

By early autumn the predictable had happened. South Africa, unsuccessful against the Cuban firepower, had halted its drive to take Luanda and finally withdrew entirely. The UNITA and FNLA forces still were in command in much of the south but were in no position to seriously challenge the MPLA superiority.

Soon thereafter, the United States Congress, looking over its shoulder at Vietnam, voted, on December 19, 1975, against any intent of further aid to UNITA and FNLA. And disavowed also any intent of supplying arms or other military aid to South Africa.

Meanwhile, the Portuguese army in Angola had remained in the country but had withdrawn from the interior combat areas and bivouacked on the coastal areas which were the first to be MPLA-controlled and out of the combat zones. This action, coupled with the continuing MPLA victories, terrified Angola's whites.

The MPLA was avowedly anti-racist, a proclaimed policy which did not entirely convince the Portuguese, and not without reason. After the announcement from Lisbon in April, 1975, that the colonies would be given their independence, white settlers in Luanda and the surrounding area had formed vigilante groups which hunted down and killed a number of known African national activists.

Memories of this and possibly of other past iniquities led to fears of an uncontrolled vendetta once the blacks were in command. From fears to panic was a short journey. Most of Angola's white settlers left towns, cities, and farm homes for the nearest port—sea or air—and fled to Portugal. The American government contributed six and a half million dollars to this airlift, organized by the Portuguese government. On November 10, 1975, the Portuguese Army followed the civilians, effecting no sort of agreement, military or political, with MPLA before they left. These twin precipitous actions by the civilian and military Europeans would seem to have seriously hampered any future attempts by the Portuguese government to exert influence of any sort over their former colony.

The day after the Portuguese Army evacuation, on November 11, 1975, the MPLA declared Angola an independent nation.

With the declaration of independence, the MPLA turned to politics and formed the Angolan People's Republic with Agostinho Neto as President and Lopo do Nascimento as Prime Minister. On November 27 the new government was recognized by Nigeria, which also offered aid. Recognition by other African nations followed.

After the active war had stopped, the Angolan government began a very real battle of survival. Although production and exports have fallen suicidally since the exodus of the white engineers and technicians, Angola is basically a rich nation, rich in minerals—diamonds ($900 million, mostly gem stones, exported in 1974), gold, iron, copper, and manganese. Oil in quantity has been found along the west coast. Agricultural products include coffee, of which the United States has been the major purchaser, tobacco, palm oil, and manioc—a plant root from which flour is made and which is a staple food for the majority of Angolans.

The government's problem, of course, is importing people with technical skills who can run her mines, businesses, and industries, and train Angolans to take their places. Schools above the primary level need to be established, and then teachers found to instruct in them. Neither the former Portuguese government nor the white settlers gave a thought to such a remote possibility as independence. The blacks were cheap hand labor. One of President Neto's first priority tasks was to import truck drivers. When a critical part of a factory or a mine broke down there was no one to repair it. The plant was simply abandoned.

For the new Angola, the chief source of revenue has been the oil in Cabinda. After independence the government assumed the ownership of all industry but worked out a royalty agreement with Gulf, which developed the Cabinda fields and continued to run them under the new regime. Texaco, which had been exploring in the Atlantic off the western shore, continued under an allied agreement.

Most observers believe that the next few years will see the Portuguese whites returning—or coming afresh—to Angola. She has long been a haven for Portugal's unemployed. It will be a different life than under the old colonial rule and there will have to be many compromises on both sides. But it can be done if the need is great enough. And they have a common language of the cities and towns, schools and industry for both whites and blacks.

CHAPTER 10

Mozambique

Vasco da gama was the third son of a noted Portuguese admiral and had, probably through his father's influence, been given the privilege of attending the school of geography and navigation established by Henry the Navigator some years back.

Da Gama had some small successes in naval operations in his country and, in 1497, when King Manuel wanted a proven leader to establish a route to India via the tip of Southern Africa—and thus to outflank the Arabs who had had a monopoly on trade along this route for centuries—the King selected Vasco da Gama (after first offering the position, gossip said, to his father and elder brother, both of whom declined for reasons of health).

It proved a good choice. Da Gama sailed from Lisbon on July 8, 1497, with a fleet of four vessels, one of them purely a supply ship, and reached St. Helena Bay on the coast of lower South Africa on November 7, lingered there for ten days and then, after six days of buffeting by wind and water, made it around the Cape of Good Hope. After a few preliminary stops he reached what is now the Quelimane River (which da Gama called the *Rio dos Bons Sinais* or River of Good Omens) on January 25, 1498.

He planted a *patrao* or stone pillar and claimed the territory in the name of king and country, calling it Mozambique. There was already an Arab settlement there; in fact, several along the coast.

Da Gama made it on to Calicut on the southeast coast of India on May 20, 1498, got a dubious reception from the locals, and left, making a triumphal return to Lisbon on September 18. On his second voyage to India in 1502, he again stopped at Mozambique. On his third voyage in 1524, he returned as Viceroy of India, duly so appointed by Portuguese King John III in a casual assumption of possession. He died on this third voyage, but the traders (and raiders) who followed, flying the Portuguese flag, continued to make Mozambique a regular port of call and continued their historical presence, faint as it was, along the Indian Ocean coast.

They had got along well with the Arabs there for a while until the Moslems found their new friends were Christians and after that the Portuguese usually had to demonstrate a superior strength of arms, which they easily had. They established forts on Mozambique Island and at Sofala on the African coast, and organized a few small settlements inland at Tete and Sena. Sometimes these settlements were new, sometimes the Portuguese simply took over from the Arabs.

Over the next several centuries there was a procession

of soldiers and settlers in and out of the country, but there was never any attempt at more than partial control until early in the twentieth century. This, in part, was due to the weakness of the parent government and in part to the strength of the African kingdoms, which resisted strenuously any real take-over efforts.

Mozambique is an elongated country lying along the coast of the Indian Ocean, deeply penetrated in its center by Malawi. It has a total area of 303,769 square miles, making it about twice the size of California, which it resembles somewhat in contour. Mozambique has a shoreline of some 1,500 miles broken by twenty-odd rivers which transverse the country and flow to the ocean. The largest of these is the Zambezi, which divides the country in half and is navigable for almost 300 miles from the coast inland.

Almost half of Mozambique's total area is taken up with the low coastal lands which rise above sea level to 600 feet. In the center of the country are the low plateaus which climb to 1,800 feet in height, and then the higher plateaus in the southwest, along the Rhodesian border, which rise to around 8,000 feet.

The largest city and capital of Mozambique is Maputo on the extreme southeastern coast, with a population of almost 400,000 people. On most maps it is shown as Lourenço Marques, its original Portuguese name. This was changed on February 3, 1976. Other major cities are Beira, Quelimane, and Nacala, all on the coast, and Tete in the northwest. The total population of Mozambique was estimated in 1974 at 9.09 million, most of whom, of course, are native Africans of Bantu stock. Other facets of the population changed radically during and after the revolt which brought independence in 1975.

The Berlin Conference agreement of 1884–85, which gave Portugal the "right to occupation and colonization" of Mozambique, looked very well on paper but was more difficult to establish in fact. Long after Portugal claimed to have the countryside under control that control was often violently and successfully challenged by native black chieftains via furious uprisings. It was not until the 1910–1920 period just before and during the first World War that Portugal was able to obtain anything like an effective grip on her reluctant Indian Ocean colony.

The occupation then followed a classic pattern. Mozambique became a captive market for Portugal's surplus products and the farmers of Mozambique were required to send their produce to Portugal to be sold at prices set in Lisbon. Due possibly to the ineffectiveness of Portugal's government rather than any real desire to adopt a liberal policy toward the colony, the Mozambique rural farming areas, especially those in the more remote areas, at first enjoyed a certain amount of decentralized control. This ended abruptly when Antonio de Oliveira Salazar assumed the power of absolute dictator of the Portuguese Republic in the early 1930s; all essence of liberalization ended. Salazar ruled Portugal and her colonies for thirty-six years with continuous policies which brought fiscal soundness to the government but had small regard for civil liberties. Salazar suffered a stroke in 1968 and was succeeded by an associate, Marcello Caetano, who continued the old themes so meticulously that the government continued to be "the Salazar regime" until it, in turn, was overthrown in 1974. The junta which overthrew Caetano was led by General Antonio de Spinola. He and other members of the junta were motivated by their conviction that something must be done to stop "the excessive cost to Portugal of continuing the repressive colonial programs in Africa."

In Mozambique the revolt did not begin until 1964, three years later than in Angola, and the first rebel successes came in the northern provinces of Cabo Delgado and Niassa. The National Armed Forces were almost always outnumbered but, as in Angola, were able to gather support from each province as they freed them from Portuguese control.

The leadership for the Nationalists, who were both guerrilla fighters and patriots, came from the Front for the Liberation of Mozambique, otherwise FRELIMO, which had been in charge of the national forces since 1962. Two of the more able of these black leaders were Samora Machel and Marcelino dos Santos, along with FRELIMO President Eduardo Mondlane, who was assassinated by an enemy bomb in 1969.

Taking a leaf perhaps from the teachings of China's Mao Tse-tung, who preached that the revolutionary was a fish which must gather strength from the sea in which it swam, the Nationalists mobilized support from the more remote towns and villages as they won control over them. They reorganized the political and social structures of the conquered provinces, established schools and, in some cases, medical centers, neither of which the provinces had seen before. They promised "a better way of life"; practically any would be better, actually. More important militarily, they picked up recruits as they went along and secured their flanks and rear by gaining the loyalty of the large rural population.

Many of the Africans went into battle with an almost religious fervor. Xenophobic at all times, they particularly hated the white men from Portugal who had made their lives miserable for generations. The blacks fought easily, sometimes almost joyously.

And since the troops of Portugal were using the NATO weapons, the Nationalists got modern military weapons, automatic rifles, light artillery, tanks, mortars, missiles, ammunition, and other supplies from their own sources—the Soviet Union, China, other Communist and some African countries. Sweden, among other "neutral" nations, sent medical supplies and ambulances in quantity.

By 1968 the Nationalists were able to push into the central provinces of Tete and Manica Sofala, and for the next five years continued to punish the war-weary and long-away-from-home Portuguese soldiers—never very enthusiastic about the war in the first place—with minor but steady gains.

The war's end finally came, and from two sources. A group of young army officers in Lisbon, tired of the reactionary and outdated leadership of the Salazar dictatorship, executed a bloodless *coup d'etat* and took over the government with the publicized view of "democrati-

zation of the homeland and decolonization of Africa."
Before the new regime got around to dilatory action, the
commanders in the field had beaten them to it, executing
a cease-fire and the planned withdrawal of all Portuguese
forces.

Independence came on June 25, 1975. FRELIMO
slipped easily from military to political leadership and
became the only legal party. Samora Machel became the
first President of the nation and Marcelino dos Santos
became Minister for Development and Economic Plan-
ning, the ranking cabinet member. There is no Vice President. There were, of course, immediate and drastic
changes in the government and an equally immediate
and drastic reduction in the number of whites living in
the country.

The new government immediately established a
strong Marxist policy, opposing any form of capitalism.
Legislation nationalized all health, legal, educational
services (as well as funeral), and further nationalized all
rented commercial and private buildings. The latter
means that firms legally incorporated in Mozambique
may own only those buildings essential for their operations and that foreign property owners not residing in
Mozambique lost all property rights without compensation.

Rather as a logical sequence, the economic situation in
Mozambique has declined drastically since independence. The new policies, plus a natural apprehension for
safety, drove out all of the Portuguese technicians and
professionals and dried up any form of foreign invest-

ment. The nation's gross national product declined 20 to 30 percent in 1974 and again in 1975. In 1976 President Machel admitted that economically his country was in virtual ruins.

Some of this is offset outside the cities and larger towns. In the countryside, most of the population make a living from subsistence agriculture. Also, more than 100,000 Mozambicans are under contract to work in the gold mines of South Africa. Sixty percent of the miners' wages are paid to the Mozambique government in gold. The government then markets the gold for three times the official rate of $42 an ounce, pays their share to the miners, and pockets the difference.

Mozambique has been recognized by most of the nations of the world, including the United States. She has a *chargé d'affaires* at the United Nations but has been slow about establishing any other diplomatic posts. American relations with Mozambique are friendly. Trade has been moderate, with exports to Mozambique in 1975 reported at $18 million and imports at $36 million. American exports have been heavy machinery, mostly earth-moving for road building, aircraft, agricultural, and communications equipment. American imports have been mostly cashew nuts.

CHAPTER 11

Zambia

UNTIL IT WON its independence in 1964, Zambia had been Northern Rhodesia, which, with Southern Rhodesia and Malawi, formed part of a triumvirate called Nyasaland, all under the colonial rule of Great Britain. Today it is a republic under the strong leadership of a president who has been able to bridge successfully the interests between his nation's various regions and ethnic groups. The country of Zambia was named after the great Zambesi River which rises on the Katanga Plateau in the northeast corner of the nation and pours its waters into Victoria Falls. Zambia normally enjoys a comfortable balance of trade, follows a strong political policy of nonalignment, with a major ambition to promote majority rule in South Africa, Namibia, and Rhodesia, all of them long controlled by white minorities. Zambia cheerfully accepts foreign aid from the West and from the East, from the United States and from Mainland China, but has political ties to neither.

Zambia also has one of the seven natural wonders of the world—Victoria Falls. During the rainy season more than a million gallons of water a second flood over the mile-wide falls and crash 350 feet into the gorge below, throwing out columns of vapor visible for twenty miles. The ancient Zambesian name for Victoria Falls is *Mosi-oa-tynya,* meaning the "smoke that thunders."

There is archaeological evidence that Zambia was populated by some type of human or humanoid half a million years ago. Further evidence indicates that the ancestors of the present-day Bantu-speaking Zambian tribes began to arrive there nearly two thousand years ago. These were Bantu-speaking people to whom the use of iron was well known and they easily conquered and eventually assimilated the Stone Age people they found in place.

The major waves of the Bantus, though, arrived in the fifteenth century and increased their number by immigration up until the early part of the nineteenth, coming mostly from the Luba and Lunda tribes of the southern Congo and northern Angola. They were joined later by members of the Ngoni tribe fleeing from the wars of the south. Over the centuries Zambia has known many invasions, peaceful and otherwise, all Bantu in origin but by members of many tribes. The result is an unusual diversity of tribes and language, more numerous even than the rest of Southern Africa.

A few Portuguese explorers may have reached the area that is now Zambia, but the first real European influence came with the famed explorer, David Livingstone, who both discovered and named Victoria Falls. Then, in 1888, Cecil Rhodes, the British entrepreneur, who was by way of being either the era's greatest benefactor or buccaneer, depending on the point of view, pursuaded Britain to let his British South Africa Company move into the area. Rhodes won concessions from the local chiefs (but did little with them), named the land Northern Rhodesia, and it was declared to be in the British sphere of influence. In 1924 it became a British Protectorate.

In 1953 Great Britain merged both Rhodesias and Malawi into the Federation of Rhodesia and Nyasaland. In the ensuing years Zambia was the center of much of the turmoil arising in Southern Africa, created by the insistence of the Africans on a greater voice in their affairs and government. This, of course, was bitterly opposed by the white minority fearing for their future should this come about—which it did, in a series of African political moves: an election in 1962 resulting in an African majority in the legislature, the dissolution of the Federation in 1963, and full independence on October 24, 1964, when the land which had been Northern Rhodesia became the Republic of Zambia.

In December of 1973 Zambia adopted a new constitution which made official the country's "one-party participatory democracy," which had been in practical effect all along.

The President is elected for five years, with strong leadership powers. Also elected for five years are 125 members of the unicameral parliament or National Assembly, with the President given the right to name as many as ten or more members if it appears to him there is a national interest imbalance. The Assembly passes the laws, which the President may veto. If the Assembly passes a piece of legislation over the President's veto he has two choices: to subside or to dissolve the Assembly for new national elections.

Although not in total conformity politically, Zambia and the United States share many points of view, including the desirability of majority rule in South Africa, Rhodesia, and Namibia and disapproval of Soviet and Cuban military interference in African affairs. On the latter point, Zambia feels even more strongly than the States. Zambia's President Kenneth Kaunda received then U.S. Secretary of State Henry Kissinger when he journeyed to Lusaka, the capital, on a peace mission in the fall of 1976.

Zambia is the third largest producer of copper, behind the United States and Canada, and is the world's largest exporter of copper, so it is only logical that her economy should be based on the metal. The giant deposits of copper sulphide were discovered in the late 1920s at Mufulira, Roan Antelope, and Nkana. The early mines were opened mostly with American capital and, although work was delayed during the worldwide depression of the 1930s, by 1935 the copper industry was fully developed, with nearly 20,000 Africans working in the mines. The skilled labor was supplied by some 4,000 Europeans. The disparagement between the pay of the two groups led to a great deal of labor trouble during the

1940s, ending in 1949 when black and white unions eventually combined into one and a prolonged strike ensued.

For several years after independence copper prices throughout the world reached record highs and Zambia enjoyed a rich economic growth. By 1970, however, and about the time the government decided to nationalize the two major copper companies—one of which was owned by American capital—prices had dropped and for a while the economy suffered. In 1973, it had recovered sufficiently for the government to acquire 51 percent of the remaining companies and at the same time to redeem for cash previous nationalization bonds.

The Zambian government has always followed a policy of using the nation's mineral wealth to advance the economic and social welfare of Zambia, both in transportation infrastructure and in encouraging agricultural development. And, of course, in social welfare and education.

For half a century before independence, the combination of outside capital and management, which had taken the lion's share of copper profits, plus the domination of political and social affairs by white-ruled South Africa, had kept Zambia internally weak. All of the great copper wealth contributed virtually nothing to the national development of the nation. The educational structure for the Africans, as permitted by white rule, saw to it that there were few black college graduates in Zambia—less than 100—when it became independent.

A year later the new government had founded the University of Zambia, started a number of technical

schools, and instituted a network of primary and second-
ary schools. Much of this was done by the Zambian government wresting exorbitant royalty rights from the British South Africa Company whose legal right to them
would never have stood up in an unbiased court.

In line with its racial policies, Zambia since independence has followed the line of reducing trade with both
South Africa and Rhodesia. In retaliation, in 1973,
Rhodesian Prime Minister Ian Smith closed the border,
shutting off Zambia's main transit routes to the sea.
Zambia immediately sought new transport routes and,
realizing it had made a serious tactical error, Rhodesia
opened the border a month later.

The Zambian government had two recourses: to return to the tender mercies of the Rhodesian government,
bowing whenever it might choose to open and close the
border routes, or to continue to seek alternate routes.
The latter decision was taken. Zambia announced the
border would stay closed and routed its transportation
lines through Angola to the Atlantic, and through Tanzania, Mozambique, and Kenya on the Indian Ocean
coast. This was more expensive and did not help
Zambia's wavering economy at the moment, but it has
permitted Zambia to implement the United Nations resolution of full sanctions against the Ian Smith regime in
Rhodesia.

Geographically, Zambia is a high-plateau country with
an average of 3,000 to 4,000 feet above sea level. A
watershed range crossing the northern part of the country is the source of two of Africa's greatest rivers, the
Congo (Zaire) which flows northward and the Zambezi

which flows to the south, creating Victoria Falls on its
way to the Indian Ocean. The temperatures of Zambia
are generally subtropical. In the winter, May to August,
they will range from 43 to 53 degrees, and in the summer, September to March, from 80 to 100 degrees, The
rainfall averages 25 to 30 inches a year, falling mostly
from October to April. Zambia has some 290,724 square
miles, making it about the size of Texas (or France, Belgium, the Netherlands, and Switzerland combined). The
capital of Lusaka has a population of 415,000. The cities
of Kitwe and Ndola are smaller.

Zambia's chief attractions to a visiting world are its
many parks and wild game preserves and, of course,
Victoria Falls, of which Livingstone is reported to have
said: "Scenes so lovely must have been gazed upon by
angels in their flight."

Zambia has adopted a policy of excluding man-made
changes and "improvements" in its parks, does sell some
big game hunting permits but limits them severely and
encourages visitors to use the camera instead of the gun.
The giant Kafue National Park (half the size of Switzerland) has pioneered a "see Africa as it is" movement in
an attempt to acquaint the visitor with a more realistic
Africa rather than a storybook-moving picture of Africa.
One move toward this goal is the creation of a traditional
village where visitors sleep in grass huts on stilts and are
given meals that copy typical African fare. It might be
noted that the menus are slanted somewhat toward
Western tastes and that the grass huts have hot and cold
running water.

CHAPTER 12

Botswana

Botswana lies almost in the geographic center of Southern Africa, covered in its majority by one of the larger deserts in the world, the Kalahari, a vast inhospitable plain.

Botswana is and has been independent since September 30, 1966. Its official language is English, its government a parliamentary democracy. It is moderately well off in diamonds, copper, and other minerals, raises and exports an impressive amount of beef, and is trying to break away from an economic independence on neighboring South Africa because it disapproves strongly of that country's apartheid policies.

Most interesting, however—and an exclusive constituent of Botswana—is the Bushman, who occupies the central portion of the 1,200-mile Kalahari and who has fascinated historians and anthropologists since the white world discovered him centuries ago.

The Bushman is small, averaging perhaps five feet two inches in height. He has a yellowish brown skin which

185

assumes a wrinkled dignity in old age. Layers of skin fold over the widely set brown eyes and tend to flatten their appearance. He is slender and stands erect.

The Bushman was once thought to have retreated as a people to the Central Kalahari to make a stand against a more aggressive enemy. Now there is a tendency to theorize that the Bushman was the original African, who actually originated in the Kalahari and, over a million years ago or so, that the other tribes all originated from him. In either event, it is doubtful if any other people in the world could live there in the Kalahari, or would try to.

The language of the Bushman (like the neighboring Pigmy in the forests of Zaire) is Khoisan or "Click," and unique to these two people. The name "Click" comes, understandably, from four sharp, implosive sounds made by the teeth and palate, plus several tones, high and low, rising and falling. (One branch of Bushman once had a fifth "click" made with the lips and known as the "kiss click" but it is little heard today.) There are scores of different varieties of the Khoisan languages, some merely dialects, some so different as to be incomprehensible to a Bushman living fifty miles away.

The Kalahari is a plateau 1,200 miles long. In the east it tends to meld into semifertile land which is suitable for stock raising. In the south it is pure sand. In the center it is a basin 3,000 feet high with an undulating surface which is covered with brownish grass and stunted bushes. It is here that the Bushman lives, along with an assortment of wild beasts which supply him food—and sometimes it is the other way around.

The climate of the Kalahari is no more hospitible than the land, with a temperature which ranges from 115 to 140 degrees Fahrenheit in the daytime, to below freezing (in winter) at night. Rainfall comes in infrequent bursts of six to ten inches and leaves moisture which the Bushman, and only the Bushman, can find—though not always—by digging in the dry *wadis* or gullies; otherwise he depends on melons and other edible plants with a high water content. These and other growths, incidentally, supply him with material for shelter, spears, and bows and arrows, along with poison for the arrows, and for any implements he may need, usually simple digging tools.

The Bushman was an accomplished primitive painter as long as two thousand years ago, demonstrating a remarkable technique with various shades, usually of red ochre, to portray in strong, clean lines the eland, giraffe, ostrich, and other animal life, including the great maned lion. The rock painting tradition, which existed up until probably six or seven hundred years ago, for some reason has been lost in more recent times.

While the true Bushman does some planting and harvesting, he is largely a nomadic hunter. His chief source of food is the eland which grazes in small bands across the Kalahari. Frequently the game is driven by beaters (women and children) into nets which may be strung over hundreds of yards and held by the men of the tribe. The real skill of the hunter comes, however, when the

Bushman, with a transcendent craftsmanship, worms his way over as much as a quarter mile of the plain, taking advantage of every shrub and shadow and frequently guided by a companion much farther distant, so that he will not have to lift his head and alarm his quarry. When he gets within bow-and-arrow range, he strikes with the poisoned arrow. Thereafter, the animal is trailed until, weakened by the poison, he collapses and is killed with a spear.

Everything edible on the animal is eaten, including the stomach which is valued equally for the moisture it contains. The Bushman cooks his food but often, if hungry enough, will eat part of it raw while the rest is roasting, and he seems to like it equally—raw or well done. In times when the hunting is good he will eat hugely— several pounds of meat at a sitting. Legendarily, his body frugally stores any excess in his buttocks for future needs.

The Bushman is a calm, friendly person. He is meticulous about sharing fairly his kill with others of his band. He marries young, has few children, and an overriding respect for his elders. Writing in the official Botswana magazine, author-photographer Alec Campbell, says: "It is his culture which permits the Bushman to survive under conditions which would speedily eliminate us. For the Bushman is at one with his environment. In understanding it, he protects it and uses it for his existence.

"The Bushman is generous, calm, good-humored and friendly; in particular he is gregarious and happiest in company.

"The Bushman believes that there is a Being who created the total environment not for the Bushman alone, but for the other animals, plants, and elements which form a part of it."

Like the rest of Southern Africa (most all of Africa, in fact) Botswana (known as Bechuanaland until independence) has no written history back of the early nineteenth century when the country was partially explored by hunters and missionaries. Through tribal tales, however, it is known that the residents were well established as herdsmen by at least the early seventeenth century and (through stone paintings) existed in the Kalahari as far back as at least the second millennium before Christ.

Except for the Bushmen who occupied the Central Kalahari, some 80 percent of Botswana's population lived, and probably always has, in the eastern part of the country. Today the country has a total population of some 700,000 (the Bushmen make up about 60,000 of this), clustered in villages which range from a few thatched huts to large settlements. Apart from the Bushmen, the Botswana are probably part of the Bantu-speaking tribes which moved in from Central Africa about the time of the birth of Christ. The language of Botswana is predominately Setswana.

Up until the early nineteenth century the villagers of Botswana lived largely at peace with one another and the rest of the world. About this time the Zulus acquired expansionist ambitions and began raiding from the northeast, while the Boers, pushing through the Transvaal, were appropriating the grazing lands of the south.

Totally unable to cope with either of these enemies, let alone both, three of Botswana's principal tribal leaders appealed to the British for help. The leader of the tribal chiefs, incidentally, was Khama III, whose grandson was to become the first President of Botswana.

The British responded and in 1885 declared the entire nation under British protection, first as a Crown Colony and later as part of the Cape Province, now part of South Africa.

While making no secret of its disapproval of neighboring South Africa's segregation policies, Botswana maintains a working relationship there because of close economic ties. The same is true of its association with Rhodesia. (Because of its geographical position, Botswana literally sits astride the strategic route across Southern Africa from east to west.)

The country's first President, Seretse Khama, came to international attention in 1948 when, as the son of the nation's most important tribal chieftain, being educated at Oxford, he married a white woman, Ruth Williams. His tribe forgave this transgression against tribal law, but local politicians and the British, both in Africa and England, didn't. As a result, Seretse Khama had to foreswear his chieftainship before returning to Botswana. This in turn led him into national politics as a plain private citizen and he, obviously, became quite good at it. The extreme bigotry of the London incident, oddly enough, did not make Khama racist, but sent him in just the opposite direction.

The Botswana government follows a policy of nonalignment internationally and has tried to diversify its contacts with both the West and East. On one hand it accepts political refugees from South Africa, Rhodesia, and Namibia, while at the same time intercepting guerrilla fighters making their way to the same countries to oppose the apartheid policies.

About 75 percent of Botswana's 719,000 people make a living through agriculture, utilizing only about 5 percent of its 220,000 square miles, all that is tillable. The country is entirely landlocked, bordered on the south and east by South Africa, on the northeast by Southern Rhodesia and Zambia, and on the west and north by Namibia. Its capital is Gaborone, located virtually on the border of South Africa, with a population of 21,000. Other and slightly smaller towns are Francistown in the northeast, the industrial center of the nation, and Lobatse, just south of Gaborone, the meat-packing center.

Some of the villages of Botswana are actually much larger than any of its designed cities, several of them approaching populations of 40,000 people. These tribal settlements have altered little throughout the centuries. They are built around the home of the chief and of the *kgotla,* the tribal meeting place.

Village life in Africa, including Botswana, is carefully organized and highly democratic. Chiefs assume their positions through right of birth, but they retain their authority through the fairness and efficiency of their rule according to tribal laws and customs. They can be removed by the elders of the tribe, who usually make up an advisory board.

Actually, the Botswana rural inhabitants frequently have three homes. First and most important is the village where they live between harvesting one crop and preparing for the next. Second, they have a dwelling of sorts on the farming lands themselves, which may be as far away as thirty miles from the central village. And third, at the cattle posts on the grazing lands, and these may be as far away as sixty or seventy miles. Largest of these villages are Bangwaketse, Bamangwato, Serowe, and Kanye.

Botswana is very interested in developing its tourist trade and has air service by Air Botswana, Zambia, and South African Airways. No visas are required of Americans. The water is potable and the U.S. State Department rates both hotel accomodations and food there as excellent. Sixteen percent of the land area of Botswana has been designated as game preserves or national parks, and there are fifty miles of paved roads.

CHAPTER 13

Swaziland

SWAZILAND IS AN independent kingdom in the southeastern section of Southern Africa, surrounded, with the exception of seventy miles, by the nation of South Africa. These seventy miles it shares as a border with Mozambique. The country is about the size of the state of New Jersey, and one of the smallest political entities in Africa.

The country's generous outcroppings of granite are estimated to be possibly the oldest visible rocks in the world—as old as three trillion years. Stone implements frequently found make it evident that Swaziland has a very ancient archaeological history, possibly extending back 250,000 years or more. Rock paintings suggest that the Bushmen and the related Hottentots were in the area as long ago as 20,000 years, along with plentiful game— elephants, giraffes, lions or leopards, impala, hyenas, and the wildebeest—some of which are still there but not so plentiful.

Much later, probably around two thousand years ago, the ancestors of the Bantu-speaking people, who later came to cover almost all of Southern Africa, brought the Iron Age to what is now Swaziland and the surrounding area. And later still, the people of the present Swazi nation, migrating south in search of better lands, settled into what was then northern Zululand where they received a most hostile reception. The Zulus pushed them back northward until about 1750 when they pulled themselves together under a collection of able leaders, consolidated themselves within their present borders, and held on.

Today there are some 382,000 Swazis representing seventy clans. The largest of these clans is the Dlamini, presently in control of the nation. The remainder of the population is made up of another 25,000 Africans of one tribe or another, 10,000 Afrikaners (white) and some 5,000 Asians, who are the traditional clerks, bookkeepers, and storekeepers of the nation.

Nine-tenths of the Swazis live in villages which are divided into homesteads. Each village has a headman, usually one of the patriarchs and, in variation with most other African civilizations, a "village mother." She frequently turns out to be the headman's mother as well, and controls all of the details of the homesteads, arranges marriages, settles minor disputes, and usually dictates details of the farming schedules. Each homestead has a cattle *kraal* and a bachelor's quarters where the young males are segregated, a common practice among African tribes.

Life in the homesteads runs along a regular schedule dictated by the seasons. Spring, from August to October, is the time of the early rains and for the planting of small gardens along the river banks.

Summer, from November to January, is the period of heavier rains and everyone turns out, even the men, to plant and hoe corn and mullet in the larger fields. Summer is also known as the "hungry season," for there is only the stored grain to depend on, if any remains. If not, it must be purchased—with money if any is available or, more commonly, by exchanging days of labor for bushels of grain.

Autumn, the two months of February and March, is the beginning of the harvest time and the early crops are brought in.

Winter, from April through July, is the time for the late and major harvest, and the time, also, for threshing the grain, some of which is eaten immediately and some stored, the quantity of each depending on the bounty of the harvest. Winter is also the time for hunting and playing, for visiting and for relaxing.

The Swazis are a musical people, gregarious, friendly, fond of dancing. Their musical instruments are rattles on both wrists and ankles, or shaken by hand, buckhorn whistles, and long reed flutes. They have songs for every occasion and for every period of life: songs for babies, for children, youth, adulthood, and for old age; for courting, for weddings, mourning, working—and for insult. There are tribal songs and clan songs.

And there are, of course, tribal and national dance

festivals. Two of the better known are the *Inciwaldi,* a rather sacred rite which represents the King as the source of power, unity, and fertility. And the Reed Dance, which encourages the unmarried maidens to be disciplined, to work in harmony, and to preserve their virginity.

This, of course, is one side of Swazi life. There is another side, too, the world of motor cars and airplanes, politics, cities, tourists, modern restaurants and hotels, and of gambling casinos.

The word "Swazi" liberally translated means "the people of Mswati," who was the first of the early and able rulers who pulled the nation together. Realizing that he could not hold out against both the Zulus, who were raiding on one side, and the Boers who were encroaching avidly on the other, Mswati appealed to the British for help and an "accommodation" was reached in 1884 which provided for the tiny nation's independence under the protection of Great Britain. For many years, however, this arrangement was a tenuous thing and the succeeding Swazi rulers found it necessary to make many concessions to the Boer settlers, ranging from giving up huge tracts of land to conferring the right to operate all bars on Swazi railroads. (To this day there isn't a mile of rail track in Swaziland.) One result of the concessions was both duplication and overlapping of land titles, with some of the disputes still in the courts today.

After the end of the Boer War, in 1903, the British formally took over the administration of Swaziland, intending eventually to incorporate it into South Africa.

After World War II, however, with the intensification of apartheid, London began having second thoughts and so did the Swazis. In 1921 Sobhuza II became *Ngwenyama*, "The Lion" or King of Swaziland after a twenty-year rule by his mother, Queen Lobatsibeni, as regent. He still ruled as this was written, a magnificent figure of a man in his late seventies.

The urban-based political parties, partly in response to political activities elsewhere in Africa, began agitating for complete independence in the early 1960s, and despite the bitter protests of the small white minority, a constitutional monarchy was organized, a parliamentary election was held, and Swaziland became completely independent in 1968. The elections and the result did not, however, prevent a continuation of bitter political infighting among various political parties, and in 1973 King Sobhuza abolished both the constitution and the Parliament and assumed to himself all governmental powers, ruling with a Prime Minister and a Council of Ministers, all of whom he appoints.

Swaziland's foreign policy is generally considered to be enlightened. In the United Nations the Swazi Ambassador vigorously opposes racial discrimination and the sale of arms to the segregated countries of Southern Africa. Refugees are accepted, though Swaziland must get along with her big segregated neighbor, South Africa.

Swaziland's major farm products are corn, livestock, citrus fruits, cotton, rice, and pineapples, its mineral resources iron ore, asbestos, and coal. Though the gross national product is only $130 million, the country has consistently maintained a favorable balance of trade and receives some foreign aid—mostly from the United States. The big and new and growing industry there is tourism, with guests being attracted to the beautiful scenery, ranging from the mountainous high veld in the west to the subtropical low veld in the east.

The country boasts excellent tourist facilities, including the Royal Swazi Spa and Casino in the capital city of Mbabane, which has a population of 16,000. There are also inns, game preserves, golf courses, horseback riding, fishing, and tennis, and between them they attract between 250,000 and 300,000 tourists annually.

Eight mineral springs rise from those ancient granite formations mentioned earlier, the spring water ranging from scalding to lukewarm, and these, like the geysers of Yellowstone, attract thousands. One of them in particular has, over the years, become a favorite spot for couples who have partaken too deeply of the fleshpots of nearby Mbabane. Reputedly highly therapeutic for the sins of overindulgence, it has become known as "The Cuddle Puddle."

CHAPTER 14

Lesotho

LESOTHO IS AN enclave entirely surrounded by South Africa, the only country in the world completely surrounded by another. Located on the highest part of the Drakensberg Mountains—which rise steeply enough from the coast of the Indian Ocean to be better known as the Drakensberg Escarpment or, literally, fortress—it is one of the highest nations in the world, ranking with Tibet in Asia and Sikkim in India.

Lesotho was called Basutoland until October 4, 1966, when it became an independent nation and changed its name to Lesotho (pronounced Le-soo-too). The people of Lesotho are the Basotho (singular Mosotho) and their language is Sethoso.

The "Father" of Lesotho is a chieftain named Moshoe-shoe (and that name is pronounced Mo-shway-shway), whom history notes as one of the great early leaders of Southern Africa in the nineteenth century.

In the late years of the eighteenth century, the tribes

in the southeastern area of what is now South Africa were victims of the "wars of calamity" brought about by the Zulu expansionist dreams. Some of those tribes were overwhelmed by the Zulu, others were scattered; then some or all were caught up in the succeeding conflict of Boer and British.

Moshoeshoe gathered up his own Basotho people and embraced the bits and pieces of other scattered tribes after a series of near-disastrous wars, and in 1868 persuaded the British to annex the little country as a colony. The move was to prevent its annexation by the Orange Free State, then independent and ruled by the Dutch settlers, or by Britain's own Cape Colony. The British drove a hard bargain by subtracting from the then Basutoland some of its better grazing ground for the Cape Colony, now the Cape Province and part of South Africa. This part of the bargain is still bitterly resented by the Basotho, but in return King Moshoeshoe extracted a provision that no white should ever be allowed to hold title to land in his country, a provision which still stands. And, of course, the British granted self-government in a step-by-step process which finally culminated in full independence.

Under the constant threat of being swallowed up by their powerful neighbor that surrounds them, the Bosotho in their high mountain kingdom have achieved a highly developed sense of survival, a sophisticated political awareness, and the highest literacy rate in Southern Africa. The government is a constitutional monarchy with the King as Chief of State and—on paper—an ap-

pointed Prime Minister and cabinet. The present Prime
Minister, Dr. Leabua Jonathan, suspended the constitution in 1970 and rules by decree. Moshoeshoe II—a
name he assumed on taking the throne—is King. The
Prime Minister accedes to the advice of an Interim National Assembly, established in 1973, which includes
representatives of Lesotho's four legal political parties.
There are discussions about writing a new constitution.
There have been a few attempts to overthrow the present
government, all unsuccessful.

About one-fourth of Lesotho's 11,716 square miles
—about the size of Maryland—lie in the western "low-
land" section, that is, from 5,000 to 6,000 feet above
sea level, and this is the main agricultural region.
Lesotho is not a rich nation in a material sense, and
most of its stationary population live in this sector
where the people farm the land. Their largest crop is
corn, which is resold to the cattle growers. Some
sorghum, wheat, beans, and peas are also grown, but
the per capita income is only a little over $100 per
person, with a zero growth rate. The population of
Lesotho (estimated) is some 1,200,000 people.

To arrive at even this income, some 200,000 members
of the Lesotho work force must absent themselves at any
given time, working in the mines and factories or on the
farms of South Africa. Though the wages they bring
home total about $25 million and constitute a large share
of Lesotho's national income, they average out at about
$125 annually per worker and to earn even this much he
must spend a fair share of his time away from home. This

is a fact of existence the Basotho people and government must put up with—but not happily.

It has been remarked that Lesotho's assets are "people, mountains, water, and scenery," and the country has been trying almost desperately to market these assets via tourism. Until recently, because of this spectacular but rugged mountain scenery, many of the nation's loveliest sites were accessible only by light airplane or the wild, sturdy little pony which is a way of Bosotho life, along with the colorful blanket used as a cloak, and the conically shaped straw hat which is so traditional that it has been incorporated into the national flag.

To develop more normal means of transport across country and into the interior, the Lesotho government has been building a network of dirt roads which are negotiable by four-wheel vehicles, usually the ubiquitous Land-Rover, one of the roughest-riding vehicles ever conceived by man. These roads were ingeniously come by through "food for work" teams, that is, a "you do the work and we'll keep you fed" arrangement which certain other nations might well study. A black-topped road from the capital of Maseru on the northern border to Thaba Tseka in the scenic center was done with Canadian aid. And a new airport is planned for Maseru with Iranian help, making it acceptable for larger aircraft.

As a result, plus promotion, Lesotho is beginning to attract more and more tourists, especially as travelers find themselves ethically reluctant to linger in South Africa. Perhaps, oddly, it even attracts many South Africans themselves. Maseru, the capital of some 30,000 people, presents itself as a sophisticated "fun city" with gambling casinos, night clubs, better-than-expected restaurants, and modern, if small, hotels, including the omnipresent Holiday Inn. All of these are almost exclusively the province of the whites, for the simple reason that the local population can't afford them.

The "season" is in the warm and mild summer, from October to June, and Maseru is the jumping-off spot to almost anywhere else in Lesotho for sight-seeing, hunting, fishing, or hiking. By American or European standards, expenses there are unbelievably reasonable. Visas may be obtained on arrival, occasional taxis are available and they drive on the left.

CHAPTER 15

Malawi

THE GREAT RIFT VALLEY of Africa is a 6,000-mile-long fissure in the crust of the earth that starts in Lebanon and travels southward. It was formed by savagely violent natural forces which tore apart the surface of the earth to varying depths, causing huge chunks to sink in some places and forcing up massive cones in others, these latter by volcanic eruption.

Thirty of the Rift's volcanoes are still active. Hundreds of others are dead witnesses to the earth's anger in the past.

Along the Rift's path are hundreds of lakes, many beautiful, some corroded into malodorous mud masses by salt or soda. Its plains, valleys, and streams contain some of the last and largest game herds left in the world and millions of birds of a thousand varieties. In the Danakil Desert of Northern Ethiopia the Rift drops to four hundred feet below sea level and surface rock temperatures have been recorded as high as 300 degrees Fahrenheit.

The Great Rift ends in the upper part of Southern Africa, shortly after creating Lake Malawi, the third largest lake in Africa. This body of clear, uncontaminated water makes up nearly a quarter of the landlocked nation of Malawi and was discovered in 1859 by Dr. David Livingstone, the Scottish physician and missionary, who also discovered Victoria Falls and whose name became a part of American folklore with the successful search for him by explorer-journalist H. M. Stanley.

Malawi has a area of 45,747 square miles, making it about the size of Pennsylvania, and is bordered by Tanzania, Zambia, and Mozambique. It and Angola are the two northernmost of the ten nations in the Southern Africa group.

The first known settlers of Malawi were the Maravi, a Bantu people who reached the shores of the great lake many centuries ago and from whom the present name derives. The first Kingdom of Maravi (about the date of 1500) was composed of the ancestors of today's two major Malawi tribes, the Chewas and the Nyanjas, both branches of the Bantu.

The Portuguese, pushing inland, were the first white men to reach present-day Malawi, but they did little more than visit. The first contact of any lasting significance came with Livingstone's arrival there in 1857. After his death in 1873, the Church of Scotland established memorial missions at Blantyre and Livingstonia.

The latter third of the nineteenth century saw Malawi in turmoil. The area was ravished by invading tribes in search of slaves, the missionaries had trading and supply problems, Portuguese claims to sovereignty resulted in intervention by Cecil Rhodes and his British South Africa Company. Finally, in 1891, the British moved in to take over the area as a Protectorate. It was, at that time, called Nyasaland.

For the next half century Great Britain accomplished a typical job of colonization. It told the Portuguese to get out; the Portuguese went. The first Commissioner then successfully subdued the raiding and warring tribes, sometimes peacefully, more often not.

And the Commissioner, one Harry Johnson, created a new economic order. He instituted new land policies which enabled those European settlers already in place to maintain established highland coffee plantations profitably and also for the new white settlers to grab off large chunks of land for nominal costs.

Johnson then instituted a taxation program designed to fiscally trap Malawians into working at zero to minimum wages several months each year for the plantation owners.

The only markets were in the south of the country. The individual Malawian farmers could sell their produce in these. The people of the north, where the farming was at a subsistence level, were forced to seek employment in the mines of Rhodesia and South Africa for any cash wages.

The Malawians lived under this traditional colonial rule, which was not as repressive, certainly, as that of many of its African neighbors, but bad enough that by the late 1950s a tremendous pressure was building up for black native control. In 1953 the white settlers were successful in achieving a long-planned connection with the nations to the south: Nyasaland was joined with Northern and Southern Rhodesia to become the Federation of Rhodesia and Nyasaland. This, however, did not stop the drive of the Malawian blacks for independence; it came ten years later.

The first President of Malawi, Hastings Kamuzu Banda, was born in Malawi in 1906, received his early education in Rhodesia, where he worked as a hospital orderly, and in South Africa, where he saved enough money for ship passage to the United States. He earned a degree in philosophy at the University of Chicago and in medicine at the Meharrary Medical College in Nashville, Tennessee. He later also studied medicine at Edinburgh University.

During and after World War II, Dr. Banda practiced medicine in England and became interested in politics after meeting other black leaders of other African colonies in London, all concerned about independence for their countries. During this time Dr. Banda began corresponding with black leaders in his own country, then Nyasaland, their chief subject being a mutual (but futile, at that time) objection to the federation with Rhodesia.

Then, in 1958, Dr. Banda returned to Malawi, with a stopover in Ghana where he practiced medicine, and took over the leadership of the Nyasaland political movement toward independence, eventually consolidating the movement into the Nyasaland Congress. Shortly thereafter it was renamed the Malawi Congress Party.

After two conferences in London and an overwhelming victory by the Party in national elections, Great Britain agreed to independence. On December 31, 1963, the Federation of Nyasaland and the Rhodesias was dissolved. On July 6, 1964, the name Nyasaland was dropped for Malawi and the country became fully independent. Two years later, exactly, a new constitution was adopted and Malawi became a republic, with Dr. Banda as its first president. In 1970 he was proclaimed President for Life by unanimous resolution of the Malawi Congress Party.

The government Dr. Banda has formed is very conservative by African standards. He has consistently courted good relations with the West and avoided serious contact with the Communist nations. He believes that the success of his nation's policies can be judged by the success of the individual Malawian. He himself has invested in farm land to employ Malawians, and has encouraged other leading Malawian figures to do the same. He has promoted friendly relations with South Africa and Rhodesia because he is almost totally dependent on them economically; they are his main trading partners on the continent and South Africa still employs thousands of his people. In 1971 Dr. Banda paid an official visit to the South African capital and a year later received the Right Honorable Balthazar Johannes Vorster, Prime Minister of South Africa, back in Malawi. Dr. Banda also has established diplomatic relations with Portugal, a unique feature for an African emergent.

Malawi and the United States have a cordial relationship. There is a small Peace Corps unit there and the

American government has assisted projects in public health, education, and transportation with aid grants totalling $54 million. Personal income in Malawi has doubled since 1964 and exports have quadrupled. Chief exports are tobacco, tea, sugar, and peanuts.

Geographically, Malawi is dominated by its spectacular Lake Malawi which measures 560 miles in length and varies from 50 to 100 miles in width. It is 1,500 feet above sea level.

To the west of the lake the great plateaus rise to 3,000 and 4,000 feet and have a pleasant and temperate climate. Farther north the peaks climb to 10,000 feet. In the south the Valley of the Shire River, which flows from the southern end of Lake Malawi, drops to nearly sea level and the temperature will rise to as high as 120 degrees in October and November, the summer season.

Malawi courts Western investors to its peaceable land, emphasizing its ample labor supply and need of managerial and technical experts willing to teach that supply of labor. It also welcomes tourists, with its great lake the chief attraction, but asks visitors to note that slacks for women are banned (except for sports at the lake holiday resorts) and skirts must cover the knees.

The capital of Malawi is Lilongwe, with 70,000 people. The largest city is Blantyre, with 170,000.

Bibliography

Berman, Robert, ed. *Diamonds.* Clarendon Press, Oxford, England, 1965.

Bissell, R. E. *South Africa, Foreign Relations.* Westwood Press, Boulder, Colorado, 1977.

Carter, Gwendolen M. *Southern Africa in Crisis.* Indiana University Press, Bloomington, Indiana, 1977.

Copeland, Lawrence L. *Diamonds, Famous, Notable and Antique.* The Los Angeles Gemological Institute of America, 1966.

Curtain, Timothy and David Dalby, Ruth First, Philip Foster, Andre Huybrechts, Ian Livingston, Geoffrey Parrinder, F. White. *Africa South of the Sahara.* Europa Publications, Ltd., London, 1977–78.

Daniels, George M. *Rhodesia Policies and Government.* Third Press, New York, 1974.

Davenport, T. R. H. *South Africa, History.* University of Toronto Press, Toronto, Canada, 1977.

Dickinson, Joan. *The Book of Diamonds.* Crown Publishers, New York, 1965.

Gibbs, James L., Jr. *Peoples of Africa.* Holt, Rinehart & Winston, New York, 1965.

Green, Timothy. *How to Buy Gold.* Walker & Company, New York, 1975.

————. *The World of Gold.* Walker & Company, New York, 1968.

Hanna, Alexander J. *Rhodesia, History.* Clarendon Press, Oxford, England, 1969.

Hoagland, Jim. *South Africa—Civilization in Conflict.* Houghton Mifflin Company, Boston, 1972. (Also Hoagland's series on Southern Africa, *The Washington Post,* 1977.)

Lewinsohn, Richard. *Diamond Mines and Mining.* E. P. Dutton, New York, 1938.

McClellan, Grant S. *South Africa.* T. H. Wilson Company, New York.

Quigg, Philip W., with foreword by Hamilton Fish Armstrong. *South Africa Race Question.* Greenwood Press, Westport, Connecticut, 1977.

Roberts, Brian. *The Diamond Merchants.* Charles Scribner's Sons, New York, 1973.

Rosenthal, Eric. *Gold, Gold, Gold.* Macmillan Company, Ltd., Johannesburg, South Africa, 1970.

TEXTBOOKS

Belasco, Milton Jay and Harold E. Hammond. *Africa, History, Culture, People.* Cambridge Book Company, Cambridge, Massachusetts, 1976.

Boyd, Allen R. and John Nickerson. *Tropical and Southern Africa.* Scholastic Book Services, New York, 1976.

Burke, Fred. *Africa.* rev. ed. Houghton Mifflin Company, Boston, 1974.

Foster, Philip. *Africa South of the Sahara.* Macmillan Publishing Company, New York, 1974.

Hapgood, David. *Africa.* Ginn & Company, Lexington, Massachusetts, 1974.

Wiley, Marylee and David. *The Third World.* Pendulum Press, West Haven, Connecticut, 1974.

PERIODICALS

The London Economist, Forbes, Time, Newsweek, U.S. News & World Report, The New York Times, The Washington Post, The Miami Herald.

United States State Department. *Background Notes.* Available on individual countries at some public libraries and at State Department Library, Twenty-second and C Streets, Washington, D. C. 20520, thirty-five cents each.

Botswana, Lesotho, Malawi, South Africa, Swaziland, and Zambia maintain embassies in Washington, D. C., with informational literature available, South Africa also acting for Namibia. Rhodesia has an Information Office only.

Index

CLARKE NEWLON is a former newspaperman, magazine writer and editor. He is the author of more than a dozen books, both adult and juvenile, including political history works on Mexico and the Middle East. His most recent title was *The Middle East —and Why.* He is also a former colonel of the Air Force and lives and works in Washington, D.C., and Key West, Florida.